The Thames Valley has an extraordinary wealth of fine architecture of many different kinds: country houses, cottages, town halls, bridges, almshouses and inns. William Collier has chosen some of the best and most characteristic examples from each period and linked them together in a penetrating and evocative narrative. He stresses throughout their connection with the life of the past, explaining how and for whom they came to be built. This combination of architectural and social history provides the reader with a clearer and fuller understanding of the buildings. Their variety and charm are fully illustrated by many photographs.

Usually recorded under separate counties, the buildings have here been gathered together in one book for the benefit of all who wish to visit and read about a region of great scenic beauty.

One of a series on the Thames Valley and the Chilterns, this book is an essential introduction for everyone who cares about the unique heritage of our countryside and country towns.

HISTORIC BUILDINGS

HISTORIC BUILDINGS

The Historic Architecture
of
the Thames Valley

WILLIAM COLLIER

SPURBOOKS LIMITED

Published by

SPURBOOKS LTD.

1 Station Road,
Bourne End,
Buckinghamshire.

S B N   0 902875 34 5

Photoset and Printed
by Redwood Press Limited
Trowbridge, Wiltshire

CONTENTS

ILLUSTRATIONS

7

Photographs by Frank Martin, or reproduced by permission of *Country Life* and the National *Monuments Record*

ACKNOWLEDGEMENTS

My thanks are due to Mrs Mockler of Milton House for her generous gift of photographs; to the National Trust for permission to reproduce photographs of the interior of Greys Court; and to the staff of the National Monuments Record for their help in providing many of the illustrations in this book.

I am particularly indebted to Mr. Nicholas Cooper for taking a series of excellent photographs illustrating the special regional characteristics of the Thames Valley's architecture. His detailed knowledge of the region has been of great help to me in discussions.

CHAPTER I
A General Survey

Variety is the keynote of architecture in the middle Thames Valley. In other regions of the British Isles one particular material, whether stone, timber, brick or plaster, is used for the exteriors of so many buildings that it largely determines the character of the region's architecture. But down the Thames from Oxford to Staines there is a succession of different local materials.

The area round Oxford has its own form of limestone, not quite as hard as the best Cotswold stone but easily quarried and carved. Lower down between Streatley and Goring the Berkshire Downs on one side and the Oxfordshire Chilterns on the other provide chalk and flints, the chalk useful for plaster and mortar, the flints for rough walling.

East of this comes an area where there is no good stone and where in the early Middle Ages most buildings were timber framed, as they were throughout the region wherever protection from risk of fire was not the first need. In the late Middle Ages bricks from local clays began to be made. Timber became scarce with the gradual destruction of woodlands in the 16th and 17th centuries, so that bricks began to be used as the usual alternative to timber in the lower parts of the valley, while in the central and western parts they were used together with flints and rough stonework.

Local materials were preferred at first because communications were so bad. The Thames, however, provided a route for barges so that good stone quarried above Oxford, at such places as Burford, could be floated downstream, to begin with, only for the most important buildings such as castles and abbeys. The river was sufficiently slow flowing in summer for loads to be sent upstream from London. These cargoes would include sawn timber. At various points the Thames barges could unload their cargoes on to waggons to take them to places not too far distant from the river.

9

With the materials from afar came the craftsmen. Masons who had learnt their skill in the stone country of the Cotswolds west of Oxford would travel east, many of them to the City of Oxford, where the construction and repair of colleges, churches and university buildings provided work for long stretches at a time. Other masons continued on down the valley to wherever good stonework was in demand, usually maintaining close links with their fellow craftsmen in Oxford and with those who stayed to work the Cotswold quarries. In the limestone districts east of Oxford there were local masons who could not only build rough stone walls, but also manage the more skilled work which included carving. Another type of local craftsman lived farther east specialising in the difficult task of making sturdy walls out of rough flints and shaped or knapped ones. Skill in brickwork began rather slowly in the lower parts of the valley and it was not until the later 17th century that good, regularly shaped bricks were made. One of the difficulties was that brick kilns were small and local, sometimes started for just one fair sized house, and higher standards spread slowly among itinerant bricklayers.

Other craftsmen who travelled the countryside included glaziers for windows, plumbers for lead roofs and rainwater pipes (drainage where provided was often by a covered brick channel) and such esoteric trades as painters and gilders. Smiths for ironwork could be found in most villages from the late Middle Ages onwards. The general rule was that the crafts not in common demand were found only in the towns and the even more scarce only in the larger towns. When needed, the craftsman would travel to carry out work within an easy distance of his home, so that a painter, for example, in the 17th century, might go from Oxford to Abingdon to undertake a particular commission.

Travelling craftsmen helped to spread both techniques and styles. The craftsman based on a town carried town styles to the country at the same time as he employed his particular skill. Similarly the masons of the later 17th century carried their craftsmanship from the middle Thames Valley to London, where they were needed to rebuild the City churches after the Great Fire. From London they returned to spread Sir Christopher Wren's version of the Renaissance style not only of Oxford but also to smaller towns and to country houses.

These craftsmen might themselves have a decisive influence on style. Generation after generation of medieval carpenters elaborated the complex and ingenious English methods of timber framework for the walls and roofs of houses. More often the craftsman acted less as an initiator of styles than as an intermediary, spreading ways of building which

met with approval for a variety of reasons.

It was the richest patrons who could best afford to experiment with new methods and since the Thames Valley had the richest of all patrons in the King at Windsor, it frequently set an example which the rest of England followed. The King's buildings were quickly emulated by neighbouring courtiers and magnates, whose horizons were wider than those of the townsman and villager, so that they were as apt to look abroad as the King for new architectural techniques and styles. Brick-work, for example, introduced from the continent, is found early on at Henry VI's foundation, Eton College, and at Ewelme on the buildings commissioned by his chief adviser, William de la Pole, Earl and later Duke, of Suffolk.

It was Elizabeth I's Lieutenant of the Tower, Sir Michael Blount, who built one of the most perfect houses in the new style of the 16th cen-tury with its Renaissance feeling for balance and symmetry. When the Stuarts introduced Baroque painted decoration into England, they chose Windsor Castle for their most ambitious project, while England's fore-most Italianate Baroque architect William Archer worked at Marlow for the 18th century politician and courtier John Wallop Earl of Ports-mouth. Even when the monarchy was temporarily in eclipse as a patron of architecture, the aristocratic coterie led by Horace Walpole employed a French artist to paint decorations in the new Rococo style of which one series was for the Duke of Marlborough at Bray. Walpole's own Rococo variant, Strawberry Hill Gothic, was soon amitated at Milton Manor House, at Padley and in the Chapel at Mapledurham.

Fashions in building also came up the Thames from London. The great increase in brick houses in the later 17th century owed much to the rebuilding of London dwellings in brick after the Great Fire. Later the stucco terraces of Regency London helped to establish a fashion for this new material lasting well into Queen Victoria's reign. Cliveden, refaced in stucco in 1850, illustrates a reverse trend from country to town, for it was Barry's grand Italianate style at Cliveden and other country houses which was copied for the stucco Victorian terrace of South Kensington and Bayswater.

There were thus two main reasons for architectural variety in the region. One was the variation in locally available materials and crafts, which continued to affect cottages and farm buildings long after the middle ages, so that even in the last century, with vastly improved com-munications, there was still a preference for the different local building materials, partly from innate conservatism, partly from conscious choice because they were thought appropriate. But for larger houses the other

1. *The Library, Milton Manor*

consideration of style and fashion was often more important. This produced a different sort of variety, altering the character of buildings not so much from one locality to another as from one generation to the next.

Many changes in the architectural styles of the past are easily recognised. But because it is easy to think of medieval society as static, or at least as changing very slowly, it is also easy to forget some of the changes that took place in medieval architecture. One innovation from abroad which can be seen in the Thames Valley is the round castle tower which the Crusaders found on Byzantine fortifications in the Near East and which French and English military engineers introduced into western Europe because they had found that it was less vulnerable to attack by battering ram or by the undermining of a small section of wall. Other importations of architectural features can be missed because they were never very widely used. Stained glass, originally a new fashion from France, can be seen in churches but very seldom, in its original medieval designs, in houses. Similarly, the taste for painted Baroque ceilings in the 17th and early 18th centuries was never widespread and the Thames Valley is fortunate in having good examples of the few that remain.

Even when new styles were generally accepted, the process could take

2. *Baroque Ceiling, Milton Manor*

an unconscionable time by modern standards. In the 17th and even early
18th centuries the independent yeomen farmers continued to use features
such as pointed arches that had been handed down from medieval
Gothic architecture. The choice between what was customary and what
was in fashion could not be resolved as easily as the choice between practical questions of building methods and materials. No one, neither the
richest nor the poorest, was ever immune from considerations of cheap-
ness or convenience. A duke was content to live in a stucco house as soon
as a stucco was invented that could take the place of expensive stonework, the farmer would build brick cottages for his labourers as soon as
these were as cheap as rough stone or timber framed ones. Equally, no
building, however humble, whether cottages, almshouses, barns or dovecotes, was regarded as unsuitable for some effort at artistic quality.

Most people, in fact, wanted the best of both worlds. They wanted
convenient buildings of good appearance, and it can be fascinating to see
how these two sometimes conflicting aims were reconciled. If the lower
Thames Valley has much Georgian architecture, this is because two
changes happened at roughly the same time. One was a practical, technical change. Bricks had become cheap, well made and plentiful in the

later 17th century, and they were well adapted to houses with the new, flat-headed, fairly narrow windows which are familiar as a typically Georgian feature. The other change was a social one. The 18th century saw a gradual but sharp decline in this part of the country in the number of independent yeomen, whose outlook and buildings were apt to be strongly traditional. The yeoman was faced, if he remained a countryman, with the prospects either of becoming a tenant farmer, or of trying to rise to the squirearchy, or of sinking to being an agricultural labourer. Whichever of these happened, either his outlook became the same as that of the gentry or he became dependant on them. Even his urban counterpart, the tradesmen of the smaller towns, had to look largely to the gentry and their tenant farmers for custom. The result was that most new buildings were designed in the new Georgian style instead of being partly in a traditional style, as in the 17th century. The uniformity of architecture echoed a social uniformity based on the predominance of the landed classes. Architecture conformed to what the upper classes thought of as the rules of taste.

Tastes, however, could change at least as rapidly as building techniques. Horace Walpole's Rococo Gothic, beginning as a fashion among a small, exclusive group, led eventually to a full scale and increasingly serious-minded revival of Gothic architecture. While the yeomen had been traditional in their ideas and way of life, the upper classes in the English countryside in the 19th century were often consciously and deliberately backward-looking. Their attempt to re-establish a traditional architecture went astray for a number of reasons. Though the Gothic Revival movement was nation-wide in its results, the main architects and artists connected with it lived for the most part in the large cities and particularly in London. They failed to take sufficiently into account the regional nature of much of the architecture of earlier times and they ignored or glossed over many of those importations from abroad which paradoxically had become part of the English architectural tradition.

The whole contribution of the Georgian period, for example, was dismissed as a temporary aberration. As a result the Gothic Revival architecture in the Thames Valley is not so much a continuation of a traditional regional style as the product of a new, national one (though there are quite a few exceptions to this general rule).

In the chapters that follow, this changing architectural scene is considered chronologically, period by period. The buildings described can be no more than a small selection because the middle Thames Valley is exceptionally rich in fine architecture. This was partly a question of what people could afford. At the time of the Domesday Book survey in

the late 11th century, Berkshire was the third wealthiest county in England and Oxfordshire the wealthiest. Tax returns show that for most of the Middle Ages at (least until the early 14th century) the Oxfordshire region continued to be the richest part of England. In addition to this practical consideration there was another less prosaic one. People have long appreciated the scenic advantages of sites near or overlooking the river. An early instance of a building with a view in mind is Elizabeth I's North Terrace at Windsor. Cliveden and Nuneham Park are outstanding among many later examples. The scenery seems also to have encouraged architects to produce some of their best work, avoiding on the one hand the sometimes excessive formality of architecture in cities and on the other the strain of fantasy which is apt to affect it in wild or mountainous country. The wooded banks of the Thames call for a mature and seemly architecture, not unimaginative nor lacking in polish, an architecture that should fit well into its surroundings and yet keep a man-made and individual quality of its own.

Wherever possible the buildings chosen for description are from among those which have been little altered or enlarged and therefore best illustrate the characteristics of one age or century. Some buildings are described which date from more than one main period because they are too important to be left out. These include Greys Court, Windsor Castle and Cliveden, which are also among those buildings with interiors that can be visited by the public. Houses open for visits are described in more detail than others. A mention of a house in the pages that follow should not, however, be taken necessarily to mean that there is public access. Buildings mentioned which are not open to the public can in most cases be seen from the road in front.

This book purposely excludes descriptions of the churches and other religious buildings of the middle Thames Valley. They will be found in a separate book in this series. It would not have been possible to do justice to both the secular and the religious architecture of the region in a volume of this size.

CHAPTER II
Medieval Architecture

Few complete medieval houses survive in the Thames Valley. So many have been much altered, or entirely concealed by later accretions that those which remain in recognisable form have exceptional interest. There is even one survival from the 12th century which is a rarity in the whole of the British Isles: Norman Hall at Sutton Courtenay, an unfortified dwelling of an age whose stone architecture we know almost entirely from castles and churches. There are also a very few Norman town houses in stone, but these had to fit into more constricted sites and meet rather different needs.

3. Norman Hall, Sutton Courtenay

At first sight Norman Hall is not a particularly impressive structure. The plan is a simple oblong, there are rough stone walls and a tiled roof which would originally have had a different form of covering, most probably wood shingles. From researches and excavations it has been established that most of the 12th century dwellings of this size in the English countryside were of timber. They had halls on the ground floor because, although more accessible to attack than first floor halls, there was always the danger of attackers setting fire to the timbers supporting a first floor hall. Since this risk of fire was less great in the case of stone built halls, some of these were raised to first floor level. In this case there is one at ground level which appears to be a direct imitation of timber halls.

In order to gain the best lighting, the dwelling house at Norman Hall was placed free of any outbuildings and with a yard on either side. For access to these two yards a door was needed on each of the long sides of the hall; the more decorated one is to the front, the plainer to the back yard where there would have been such extra buildings as the kitchen, the brew house and the barn. These were probably of timber and there was thus an extra reason, that of fire risk, for keeping them separate from the hall and its wooden roof structure.

There are several interesting features to the house. On the front doorway are bands of stone ornament which resemble those on Norman church doorways. They are known by the descriptive names of dogtooth, roll and nailhead mouldings. The term moulding can be misleading because the bands are in fact carved but an architectural moulding signifies a band of a particular shape or pattern, which can be formed in various ways and is not necessarily moulded, in the sense of having been made in a mould. Fascinating though it is to trace the use of these patterns on many different types of 12th century buildings, the most significant part of the house is undoubtedly the timber roof structure. It stands at the beginning of a development which was unique in Europe, for only in England was a native skill in roof construction to make such remarkable advances. Already at Norman Hall the simple device of tying together the two sides of the roof with beams had been improved, since under the beams are curved supporting timbers known as braces which have been added to provide extra strength. The rafters as well have been given additional strengthening in the form of curved timbers laid across them known as wind braces, from their function of preventing the rafters from bending or breaking under the force of strong winds.

For lighting the hall depended on the narrow, pointed arched windows known as lancets, a type more easily made in thick, heavy walls than wider windows, which require either strong lintels or carefully built

arches. Wider windows were in fact inserted later but the original ones survive inside as deep niches. A wing has also been added to the house. It remains comparatively unaltered because the Courtenays, to whom King Henry II gave the manor of Sutton not long after the building of its hall, hastened to erect a grander Manor House, choosing not the same site (as usually happened) but one nearby. Here there is another medieval hall, but embedded in a Jacobean house that was built round it.

4. *Manor House, Sutton Courtenay*

Few substantial houses remain from the 14th century. One that has been much altered but retains some interesting features is the former rectory at Marlow which stands on the east side of Saint Peter's Street and was later divided into two dwellings, Deanery House and The Old Parsonage,—parsonage in the old sense of the term meaning a rectory as distinct from a vicarage. Marlow, lying south and east of the Chilterns, has as its nearest available building stone the hard chalk known as clunch. This was quarried from below the top layers of chalk, since these are liable to have been affected by cold and damp and in consequence to have become softer and more powdery. It may surprise people from districts with really hard stone to discover that chalk is used for the outside walls of buildings and indeed it would not be a durable material in the atmosphere of most towns or at the bases of walls exposed to constant

dampness. In the right conditions, however, it can last for centuries, as the old Parsonage shows. There one can see window surrounds and tracery of clunch (one tall traceried window is visible from the road). The work dates from the mid 14th century when finely carved, curving window tracery was the current style. Clunch is well suited to elaborate carving provided the stonework is either inside or has been given some protection. The windows in Saint Peter's Street are in a sheltered position and may in earlier times have had projecting roof gables above them, but the surfaces, especially at the heads of the windows, are at last beginning to wear badly and the horizontal stone bars, or transoms, lower down have had to be renewed.

5. *The Old Parsonage, Marlow*

Inside is a hall, now partly divided up into a number of rooms. The roof, still largely unaltered from the 14th century, is an improvement on the early, simple type with just a succession of beams stretching across. Instead of the curved supports or braces that were used at Norman Hall, the beams are each joined to a solid timber arch, pointed in the centre, to make a stronger and more rigid roof. As further strengthening a post, known as the crown post, stands above and is pegged into the centre of each beam, and from this post a number of lengths of timber branches out to support the upper part of the roof. Medieval builders soon discovered that two posts on a beam were better than one, distributing the

19

load instead of concentrating it, and from there it was a short step to the late medieval hammer-beam roof where the centre of the beam and arch are missed out altogether.

6. *Ockwells Manor, near Bray, Berkshire, before reconstruction*

To find a little altered manor house of the later middle ages we must go to Ockwells near Bray. This dates from the 1460s, and was built for John Norreys, who in addition to being Lord of the Manor was an important official at the court of Edward IV. His house, while not departing from the basic pattern of the time, is rather larger than most, probably better built and certainly more luxuriously fitted. It was originally less ornate then now, after restoration early this century, as a comparison of the photographs taken before and after clearly shows. But the essentials have not been falsified. The large rectangular hall with its open timber roof is still the main feature and indicates a strong element of continuity with earlier houses. No longer, however, does the hall stand alone. At one end a wing has been added at right angles for the owner and his family, with a parlour on the ground floor and a room above known as the solar. A second wing stands at the opposite end and between this and the hall lies a passage, entered from the forecourt by way of a porch and leading through to a small courtyard where it carries round two sides in the form of an arcade.

Two unusual features distinguish this courtier's house. One is the pierced carving of the woodwork on the gables in a graceful flowing pattern; the other the stained glass in the hall windows. Window glass was

7. Pierced gables and stained glass, Ockwells Manor

becoming less of a rarity in the second half of the 15th century, taking the place of oiled cloth, thin sheets of horn or simple wooden shutters, but stained glass was still a luxury for houses, if less so for churches. Here the glass takes the form of panels displaying shields.

It is not perhaps generally realised that most,—some authorities would say all,—medieval stained glass in England was imported from the continent. Much came from Nothern France, where the particular form of fine sand needed for its manufacture was readily available, notably at Fontainebleau. The Low Countries and the Rhineland also developed centres for making stained glass and this too came to be exported to England. The glass at Ockwells is thus an early example of a building material brought to the Thames Valley from abroad (a later importation was Italian marble for chimneypieces).

8. Doorway, Ockwells Manor

There are three subjects for the stained glass panels. All of them represent armorial shields but they are divided into those of his family, of the king and queen, and of other courtiers. Sir John Norreys' motto is given as "Feyth fully Serve" and the panel also shows his badge of office, three gold distaffs, denoting the Keeper of the Wardrobe. This detail helps to fix a date for the glass, which must have been made about 1455–60, when

he was both Master of the Wardrobe and an Esquire of the Body to King Henry VI. The King's shield is that of Henry VI and the Queen's that of his wife Margaret of Anjou. Among the courtiers or court officials whose shields are shown are the Duke of Warwick, who was Hereditary Pantler to Henry VI, the Constable of England the Duke of Somerset, and Queen Margaret's Chamberlain Sir John Wenlock, a particular friend of Sir John Norreys and mentioned in his will. Another royal official included in this group is Richard Bulstrode, who was a nephew of Sir John and like him, served both the Lancastrian and the Yorkist dynasty, acting first as Keeper of the Wardrobe to Henry VI's Queen Margaret and later as Comptroller of the Household to King Edward IV.

A date for this work in the later 1450s also suggests the names of two possible craftsmen. Sir John might have employed a certain John Grayland or else John Prudde, who as the King's Chief Glazier was at that time working not far away on the new royal foundation of Eton College. Although by the later 15th century there were trained English craftsmen to fit stained glass windows, the technique and material were still novel enough to be accorded a special role in the house, as shown by their place in the great hall and by their personal references to the family of the owner and the owner himself. One finds in other subsequent houses that the latest, most valued techniques are often invested with this personal quality, so that wrought ironwork, ornamental plasterwork and even fine brickwork are to be found proclaiming the owner's initials or monogram, sometimes proudly in conjunction with the date when his house was built. The present age has transferred this assertion of individuality to car number plates.

Manor houses were not by any means the only secular medieval buildings to have good timber framework. The same carpenters who built the great houses were also employed on more strictly practical structures such as the large medieval barns, a number of which survive in the Thames valley. The great 15th century Tithe Barn, for example, at Waterside House, Drayton Saint Leonard, has an elaborate system of posts and beams carried out in massive oak timbers. Its long central space is divided into six sections or bays by the beams spanning it and on either side of the centre are narrower aisles. The whole effect seen from one of the corners inside the barn resembles that of a most carefully arranged and geometrically exact forest.

The great stone barns are often more impressive from the outside. At Church Farm in Great Haseley the Tithe Barn, dating from the 14th century, has as many as seven bays which are marked by a sequence of buttresses that strengthen the tall walls at the points where they have to

23

9. *15th century Tithe Barn, Drayton St. Leonards, Oxfordshire, note posts and beams*

take the extra weight and thrust of the roof beams. These might otherwise push the top of the wall outwards. Entry to the barn is through a tall, wide archway with a carved stone moulding running round it and a bold roof gable built up overhead. The size of this barn gives some idea of the space needed to hold the contributions in kind made by the farming community to the parish clergy, though it is in this case not the whole space that was required, for the barn was originally several bays longer.

Corn was often better housed in the middle ages than were the peasants. Few of their cottages have survived but among those that have are some constructed in an unusual way which once seen can easily be recognised. An early and simple method of forming a timber framework was to take two pairs of tree trunks, each pair secured together near the top, and suspend a ridge pole between them. From this pole was hung a network of thatch, strengthened by further horizontal timbers, to provide a shelter like a long tent. Such in essence was the origin of cruck cottages, each pair of tree trunks being known as a cruck. To give more headroom it was best to have the trunks curving in near the top, and to

24

10. *Cruck cottage, Harwell, Berkshire*

make sure that the curves were equal a trunk would be split in two, each half forming one side of the cruck. The base of the trunk might be sunk into the earth or, to prevent it decaying, placed on a low stone wall.

Most cruck cottages that remain are to be found in the central and western Midlands. A few still exist in the middle Thames Valley, as for example at Harwell, Steventon, Drayton, Lower Radley, Warborough and Long Wittenham. Those at Harwell are particularly valuable survivals because we know from Middle Farm there, built in the 14th century, that the more sophisticated form of timber framing based on upright posts and triangular roof trusses existed side by side with at least one cruck barn and with several cruck cottages. Radiocarbon tests of the timbers of these cottages have enabled estimates to be made of their ages, which vary from early 15th century to about 1600. Whereas many crucks elsewhere have been concealed outside by later protective plaster, some of these at Harwell are still exposed to show how a peasant's dwelling would have looked in the Middle Ages.

A good example is the Barley Mow, public house at Clifton Hampden. By contrast, a most ambitious group of late medieval buildings sur-

11. *The 14th century Barley Mow Inn, Clifton Hampden, a cruck construction*

vives at Ewelme. The Earl of Suffolk, William de la Pole, and his wife Alice Chaucer, granddaughter of the poet, lived here in the reign of Henry VI in a palace which has long since been pulled down. There remain, however, the School, School House and Almshouses which the Earl had built in a mixture of brick, stone and timber. For the most part the outside walls are of red brick, a fairly new fashion in the middle Thames Valley and so combined with stone in many places, in particular for the more intricate moulded surrounds to the windows. The School, for instance, has small stone window arches under the traditional stone dripmoulds, which were partly decorative, partly a protection against moisture seeping down onto the window itself. Stone is used inside for the staircase and the double entrance doors, once in the church, have delicate arched panelling resembling stone window tracery. This borrowing by carpenters of the forms used by masons can be seen again in the graceful timber roof with its beams curving up to make arches.

The School is connected to the School House by a wall of ragstone, an early example of a material imported from a quarry some distance away and probably brought up the Thames by barge to the nearby town of Wallingford. There have been quite a few alterations to the School House, such as later windows and a small Georgian chequer brick wing,

12. *The 15th century School House, Ewelme*

27

but the gable to the south has the rather mannered stepped form pictur-
esquely known as the crowstep or corbie gable.

Between the School House and the Church (rebuilt for the Earl) stand
the Almshouses, completed in 1442. A hollow square in plan, it has a
timber arcade round its central paved courtyard, some of the inner walls
filled between the timbers with bricks in herring-bone pattern, a device
which spread in the next century as bricks came into more general use.
Another anticipation of the Tudor style is the series of tall brick chimneys. In the cut brick tracery of the north doorway one can see another
example of masons' methods of building continued in the newer material.

Brickwork in central England was indeed an innovation. It had been
used only a decade earlier on buildings in the eastern counties, notably
in East Anglia, and it is thought that the workmen here at Ewelme may
have come from the de la Pole estates in Suffolk, where they had a castle
at Wingfield. Ewelme had come to William de la Pole through his marriage with Alice Chaucer and the different families connected with the
place can be traced in the shields of arms which appear both in the
stained glass of the church and carved on the outer wall of the School.
There the windows have mouldings in stone to their lintel heads, which
end either side of the windows in small figures holding armorial shields.

13. *Armorial windows, Ewelme School*

14. Door, Ewelme School

29

One shield carved with three wheels denotes the family of Phillippa Roet, the wife of the poet Geoffrey Chaucer and grandmother of Alice; another bearing three leopards' faces denotes the de la Pole family; a third with a double tailed lion belongs to the family of Burghersh. It was Maud Burghersh, mother of Alice Chaucer, who brought the manor of Ewelme to her husband Thomas Chaucer, the Member of Parliament for Oxfordshire.

The shields might lead one to think that these were ancient families proud of their lineage. But heraldry then as later in English history could lend an aura of respectable antiquity to families which had only recently risen from the ranks of the merchants and clerks. Alice's grandfather had been, in modern terms, a successful civil servant, the de la Poles had gained estates and a knighthood from lending money to Edward III, money which came from trade. They had done very well out of the Hundred Years War. It was as natural for these new rich to insist on their status as it was for them to patronise new methods of building.

The brickwork should not be looked at in isolation. It needs to be seen in conjunction with the other materials, acting sometimes as a constructional background to the carving in stone and wood. Though the School doors are very fine and bear comparison with the 15th century vestry door of the Church, the most intricate wood carving is to be found on the pierced boards fronting the courtyard gables of the Almshouses. These

15. *Almshouse porch gable, Ewelme*

30

are not yet in the flowing branch patterns peculiarly suited to woodwork, but in a series of half circles filled with smaller pierced circles and curves, a type of decoration which closely follows stonework. Altogether the Ewelme complex of charitable buildings is a fascinating blend of old and new styles and materials, comparable with the foundations of the Earl's sovereign, Henry VI.

16. *The Quadrangle, Eton College*

One would like to know how far the King was influenced by Suffolk in his foundations of King's College at Cambridge and of Eton College. Suffolk was gradually gaining an ever greater ascendancy in the royal counsels and his aim was to reduce English commitments abroad fighting the French and to concentrate instead on prosperity at home. Himself no mean poet, he was a friend of learning who would have approved the King's foundation of a school at Eton. Though much of the college is of later date, the north side of the main Quadrangle was built in the 1440's and 1450's, while the east range was constructed in a rather similar style in about 1516-20. They were both of red brick dressed with stone round the windows and doors.

The designer is sometimes given as Roger Keyes who was in fact a cleric and only responsible for supervising the master mason, Robert

Westerley, who is recorded in 1452 as being entitled to two stags yearly from Dartmoor for his good services at Eton. He had been in charge there since 1441, going in June that year to Oxford and Burford in order to recruit masons for the work. There was also a warden of masons who undertook much of the administrative work. For some of the time this office was held Robert Janyns, who had earlier held a similar post at All Souls College, Oxford, under the master mason Richard Chevynton, who was generally away supervising the quarries at Burford. It was a grandson of Robert Janyns, Henry Janyns, who acted as the chief mason for the Chapel of Saint George at Windsor, begun in 1475.

Provost's Lupton's Tower at Eton marks the entrance to an inner courtyard. It has the air, with its battlemented roof, of a castle gate-house, though it serves no defensive purpose and is rather an example of that self-conscious impressiveness which went with the tournaments and elaborate heraldry of the late Middle Ages. The artistic effort that had

17. *Brickwork detail, Eton Cloisters*

earlier been devoted mainly to churches could now, because there was less need to consider problems of defence, be turned to secular buildings.

Upper School at Eton is described in the chapter on Stuart architecture.

The Almshouses of Christ's Hospital at Abingdon were built not long after those at Ewelme. Their history, however, is very different, being closely linked with the life of the town. This fact eventually resulted in a marked difference in the character of the buildings. They back onto the churchyard of Saint Helen's and it is with the parishioners of this church that the charity originated. It was known as the Fraternity of the Holy Cross after the medieval legend by which Helen, mother of the Emperor Constantine, rediscovered the true Cross buried in the Holy Land. After various donations, in particular two large ones from wealthy, childless

men, the fraternity grew rich and received in 1441 a royal charter. This put its affairs on a more formal basis and gave it an influential head in the person of William de la Pole, Earl of Suffolk and one of the foremost royal counsellors, a useful protector at court.

One of the principal duties enjoined on the Fraternity by the Charter was to look after "thirteen poor sick and impotent men and women". It was in fulfilment of this obligation that the Long Alley Almshouses were built, being completed in 1446. There are single rooms for each occupant with doors opening into a covered passageway. Since the early 16th century this passage has had narrow window arches carved in oak, but the original openings would very likely have resembled those at the Ewelme almshouses in having more widely spaced wooden posts ending in the flattened type of pointed arch known as a four centred arch, from the four compass points from which its curves are drawn. The designer is not known but he may well have been the same as that of the Ewelme almshouses.

With the Reformation the Fraternity was dissolved. Yet only six years later, in 1553, a new charity was founded under the title of Christ's Hospital to carry out some of the practical tasks which the old Fraternity had undertaken, such as the upkeep of town bridges, administration of poor relief and the continued support of the twenty-six almsfolk. Although some properties had been sold in the interim period between the dissolution of the old charity and the foundation of the new one, there was enough property left to keep the Almshouses in good order. By the early 17th century the Governors of the Hospital had sufficient funds to enable them to add three porches elaborately ornamented by an Oxford joiner with wood carvings of "satyrs and antiques". The "antiques" probably refers to what would now be called grotesques, or fanciful carvings including real or mythical animals. Unfortunately the carvings have disappeared. However the paintings with which the porches were also decorated still for the most part survive. These were by an Oxford painter, Sampson Strong, there being no sufficiently skilled artist in Abingdon. It must be admitted that the standard of painting even at Oxford was not very high and the chief interest of the panels lies in their representation of the almsfolk and in the fact that this was thought a suitable form of adornment for the building. They are probably not unlike the inn signs of the period and would have struck the townspeople among the Governors as entirely appropriate.

At the same time a little domed turret was added to the centre of the roof. For this work and that on the hall of the almshouses a number of different craftsmen were needed and it is interesting to see which could

18. *Central porch, Long Alley Almshouses, Abingdon*

To doe good and to distribute forget not: for with such sacrifice God is well pleased. Heb. Chap. 13. Verse 16.

19. *Painting on centre-porch, Long Alley Almshouses*

be provided from among the townsmen of Abingdon and which had to come from Oxford. For the lead covering of the small dome on the lantern turret, the Governors had to send to Oxford for the plumber George Rutland, but the gilding of the weathervane could be carried out by John Bell, a local craftsman. The lantern turret that is seen today dates only from 1707, when the old one had to be renewed, but is a copy

20. *Brick Alley Almshouses, Abingdon*

35

of the first design. A stone bay window added below to light the hall was by a local mason, Lawrence Smyth, whose charge for the work was £7. Oak panelling to line the hall was brought ready sawn by barge from London as far as Culham, where it was unloaded and taken to Abingdon overland. A local joiner, Harry Becket, fitted the panels round the room.

By one of those odd anomalous compromises of English life, the Governors of Christ's Hospital were empowered in 1613 to administer the income of another smaller charity which had almshouses nearby in what is now Brick Alley, but they only became the owners of the charity's various properties much later, in 1837. Meanwhile, however, they found that the almshouses, which had been erected as early as 1417, were becoming dilapidated, so they proceeded to order a complete rebuilding. There is no record of any architect being employed. The mason, Samuel Westbrooke, may have designed them himself, since by 1718, when the rebuilding took place, there were many examples of well designed new houses in the town to act as models.

The medieval foundations survived into and were embellished by later centuries. It is now time to look at the next period.

CHAPTER III
The Tudor Period

The Tudor period of peace after the troubled times of the Wars of the Roses saw a great rebuilding throughout most of England of all types of dwellings,—manor houses, farmhouses, houses in villages and towns. With communications still difficult and transport of building materials costly, the majority of these houses in the middle Thames Valley were constructed of the good local limestone, easily quarried for rough walling and soft enough to be carved into decorative mouldings round doors and windows.

One example, altered and enlarged but keeping much of its original 16th century character, is Cromwell House at Marston near Oxford. Here Oliver Cromwell and General Fairfax met in May, 1645, and from here Fairfax organised the siege of Oxford, receiving the city's capitulation a year later. The house is a substantial one, solidly constructed in the thick rubble stonework which requires accurately trimmed stone round the door and window openings. The large stone block over the door has to take a heavy load from the stone wall above. As limestone fractures fairly easily, the block is tall in its proportions and the arch of the doorway is flattened so that the topmost point of the arch does not encroach too deeply and weaken the stone. The mason thus provides an expanse of smooth stone in one of the most noticeable places on the front wall just above the entrance. In this instance he has resisted the obvious temptation to ornament the surface with carving, contenting himself with a projecting moulded band,—the dripmould,—perhaps he was intent on carving the brackets higher up the wall which support two bay windows under prominent stone gables.

Some effort and expense were also deflected into the decoration of the interior of the house, where there are heraldic tiles with the arms of the Croke family, the then owners. Stone slates, with which the house may originally have been roofed, can still be seen on a barn to the right

beyond another dwelling which was originally part of Cromwell House.

At Brightwell Baldwin stands another interesting stone village house which later became the Lord Nelson Inn. On the front and sides it incorporates stone and wood carving which probably came from Brightwell Manor, burnt down in the 18th century, and in its general arrangement of a wide central block flanked by two gabled wings the house is a direct

21. *Cromwell House, Marston near Oxford*

22. *The Lord Nelson Inn, Brightwell Baldwin*

development from the earlier manorial plan of a hall with rooms at either end. A feature distinguishing these Tudor houses from earlier ones is the new profusion of chimney stacks and wall fireplaces. Here the main fireplace of the central block is emphasised by a carved panel showing the twelve apostles.

For really ostentatious chimneys one must go to the Manor House at Toot Baldon. It has three brick clusters of shafts set diagonally on massive stacks. Where these stacks project, almost as separate structures, from the main stone walls of the house, one can see clearly how chimneys came as an afterthought, an innovation to be tacked on to something otherwise complete.

Now that bricks were accepted even in the limestone country of the middle Thames as an equally good walling material, one begins to find many different ways in which the two are combined. At Lower Park Farm, Beckley,—an important house that belonged in the 16th century to Lord Williams of Thame,—there is a tall stone base of rubble enclosed at the angles by dressed or trimmed stone quoins. Above this on a carved stone moulding rests a brick wall ornamented by square diaper

23. *Tudor Manor House at Toot Baldon, note chimneys*

40

patterns in darker brickwork. Diapering, with the square outlines placed on end to resemble diamonds, seems to have come to England from northern France in the 15th century. There is more of it to be found in south eastern England than farther west but the pattern was always easy to make provided there were enough bricks rather more burnt in the kiln than the rest so that they turned a noticeably darker colour.

The windows at Lower Park Farm are outlined in stone. So is the doorway, with the result that the general effect is one of contrasting colours and textures. Some of this variety may be unintentional because the rough stone base may represent the remains of an earlier, medieval house inhabited for a time by Richard, younger brother of Henry III, before he built another house for himself nearby. The three moats suggest a medieval inhabited site, since such elaborate defences were no longer needed in this part of England in Tudor times.

Lower down the Thames, farther away from good building stone, the Blounts who commissioned Mapledurham House chose the newly fashionable brick as their chief material. Royal palaces such as Hampton Court and Saint James's had given brickwork social prestige. At Mapledurham it is used to great effect in conjunction with a carefully balanced design, much of the front being decorated with diapering in lighter coloured bricks. The porch is placed centrally, instead of at one end of the hall where it would have spoilt the balance of the composition,

24. South front, Mapledurham House, Oxfordshire

and the battlemented roof parapet is emphasised at this point by a gable with tall stone pinnacles. There are gabled wings at either end and tall bay windows nearly midway between wings and centre. Perhaps the most striking element in the design is the ingenious symmetry of the great brick chimneystacks, one either side of the entrance in the likeness of wide buttresses, others at the very ends of the long roof bringing it decisively to a full stop. Though each separate feature in this stately, harmonious design is traditional, carrying on from later medieval houses with no trace of Renaissance ornament from abroad, the overall effect is quite novel and essentially Elizabethan in its feeling for a new form of beauty.

Mapledurham owes its unaltered external appearance to long ownership by the Blount family. As so often with country houses of any size, it needed more than hereditary lands to pay for the building. Fortunately for Sir Michael Blount, his cousin Charles Lord Mountjoy, had attracted the attention of Queen Elizabeth I and in 1590 Sir Michael found himself appointed Lieutenant of the Tower of London. Subsequently in the 17th century the family's conversion to Roman Catholicism automatically excluded it from public office and without additional sources of income the Blounts were prevented, even if they had wanted to, from enlarging or rebuilding their house. By the early 18th century, when so many country houses in southern England were being remodelled or refaced, the Blounts had become part of that small, interrelated world of the English Roman Catholic gentry.

Their somewhat isolated lives, cut off by a different religion from the outlook and many of the occupations of their neighbours, may well have turned their attentions inwards to their house, and particularly to its interior, with its private Roman Catholic chapel and its library. Alexander Pope, the lifelong admirer of Martha Blount, in his *Epistle to Miss Blount on leaving Town* wrote:

"She went to plain work and to purling brooks,
Old-fashioned halls, dull aunts, and croaking rooks,
She went from opera, park, assembly, play,
To morning walks and prayers three times a day."

Though the family was not averse to some redecoration, there was much of excellent quality which they wisely kept. This included a whole conspectus of Elizabethan and 17th century decorative features in different techniques: fine panelling, an elaborate staircase, highly ornamental plaster ceilings and ceiling borders, or friezes, and several well carved chimneypieces.

25. Chimney piece, Mapledurham House

43

Of these the panelling is the more ordinary. It has the compensating advantage of allowing the visitor to examine characteristic woodwork of the Elizabethan period which is also well executed. The wood used throughout is the native English oak, lending itself best to carving in low relief rather than the high relief and undercutting which became fashionable in softer woods later in the 17th century. An architectural treatment is used on the overmantels of two ground floor rooms, one a private sitting room and the other the hall. In both cases there are squat pilasters (like flattened columns) which stand above bands of woodwork ornamented with plain bosses. In the sitting room two of the panels between the pilasters are filled with finely carved arches on further, smaller pilasters, while the central panel has a minute archway within a broad, flat frame. All three arches are, of course, dummy ones filled with panelling.

This whole system of larger and smaller pilasters and arches can be traced back ultimately to Italy, where it had been fashionable in a rather more complicated form well over a century earlier. How slowly fashions spread in those days is shown by the fact that it took so long for this particular one to travel from central and northern Italy across France and Germany to the Low Countries and thence, by way mostly of woodcuts in pattern books, to southern England. On the way the style underwent some changes, losing the scenes in different coloured woods which occupied the central spaces of many Italian panels in the later 15th century and gaining the decoration known as strapwork. This appears on the pilasters in the hall and is so called from its resemblance to interlacing leather straps.

In the floor of an oak panelled bedroom is a small trapdoor. It leads to a secret hiding place from which a shaft descends to a passage. A rope hanging in the shaft allowed anyone wishing to escape from the house to go quickly down and along the passage to an exit outside the house near the river, where a boat would be kept moored in readiness. Panelled rooms lent themselves to this kind of device, which is found in houses of the late 16th and early 17th centuries more often than in those of earlier or later dates. Earlier houses were better secured, by such means as gatehouses and moats, from sudden incursions and later ones built in less troubled times had no longer so much need for secrecy.

Hiding places of this kind are usually associated with the houses of the Roman Catholic gentry and it is true that there were both fewer hiding places and fewer Roman Catholics in the Thames Valley than in the west and north of England. But the fact that in the west of Oxfordshire the home of the Parliamentarian Lord Say and Sele, Broughton Castle, has a hiding place suggests that they were a natural recourse for any one

44

26. *Trapdoor to priests hole, Mapledurham House*

of standing who opposed the government and feared sudden arrest.

The main staircase at Mapledurham is also of considerable interest. Though most of the woodwork is good and some excellent, it is the general arrangement which differs radically from that of most medieval stairs, relegated to the cramped spaces of corners and turrets. At Mapledurham House the staircase spreads out round a rectangular central space, or well, and offers a leisurely ascent on broad treads and shallow risers. The wooden framework of flights and landings is supported round the well by slender columns resting on newel posts. Lord Burghley would have desbribed the staircase as offering (as he wrote of Sir Christopher Hatton's stairs at Holdenby) a "stately ascent"; and this was

27. Main staircase, Mapledurham House

46

now desirable because instead of a great chamber opening out of the hall on the ground floor, there was often one on the first floor, where there might also be a long gallery. For good measure the main stairs at Mapledurham continue right to the top of the house, where they are still carefully ornamented with carved wooden vases of fruit on the newel posts, a fashion which carried on well into the mid 17th century. The wall panelling of the staircase appears to be of a later date at the turn of the 17th and 18th centuries.

28. *Ceiling detail, Mapledurham House*

The plasterwork is perhaps the finest thing in the house. It provides a rich and lively decoration for the ceilings of the staircase and of several rooms. Their main patterns are geometrical but of two rather different types. The stairway ones have sharply raised and moulded narrow bands dividing the surfaces into areas like diamonds and pointed leaves, with rich patterns kept separate from the borders. Two rooms, one on the ground floor, the other the great chamber on the first, have ceilings which are a variant on this type. The surfaces are still divided into geometrical areas, but some of these are just those left over round the main areas, which are either circles, or squares with a semicircle added in the middle of each side. In the middle of the main areas or panels are raised

47

29. *Ceiling detail, Mapledurham House*

30. *Great Chamber ceiling, Mapledurham House*

48

plaques, some of them bearing profiles as on coins or medallions. There is further ornament on the borders, which show trailing vine branches with leaves and grapes. Round the edge of the great chamber ceiling runs a much later frieze of alternating shells and honeysuckle. The other frieze has rather formalised curving branches with leaves and flowers. All these ceilings have great charm and inventiveness. It is not to belittle them in any way to say that some of the ideas used derive ultimately from abroad, the profiles, for example, from Italian Renaissance copies from the ancient Romans.

After this the small chapel comes as something of a surprise. It was decorated in the Gothic style of the 18th century which, though pleasantly light in both colouring and form, is nowadays hard to take seriously, because Victorian Gothic has made us aware of the more powerful and sombre side of this architecture. It requires an effort of the imagination to understand the minds of people who thought this flimsy, almost frivolous style suitable for a chapel. The name Strawberry Hill Gothic, from Horace Walpole's villa in the style at Strawberry Hill, indicates exactly the flavour.

Other rooms redecorated in the late 18th century are more serious. The dining room in particular achieves its austere but elegant effect by concentrating attention on a very few features, such as the simple niches for statues and the finely carved marble chimneypiece. After the pictorial qualities of English decoration in the late 17th and early 18th centuries, this exemplifies a return to carving as the dominant element, even if some of the carving is only simulated in plaster. The interior of Mapledurham House is thus fortunate in combining work from two periods when form in decoration was often more important than colour.

Symmetrical design spread from Mapledurham and its like to smaller houses. The next step down the social hierarchy was the average sized manor house, larger than a farmhouse and with a greater sense of formality to which the new, balanced compositions were well suited. Smalls House at Brightwell has a neatly contrived plan in the shape of an H. This is emphasised by matching facades on opposite sides of the house, so that east and west fronts form one similar pair, north and south fronts another. By giving each front two large gables the builder provides an important recurring feature that goes right round the house. A further way of binding the design together is the use of continuous lines of stone mouldings, one at eaves level just above the first floor windows, the other one over the ground floor, stepping up over each ground floor window. Earlier masons usually limited these mouldings to the window heads as a practical device to keep moisture from running down directly onto the

49

31. Smalls House, Brightwell

32. Interior window, Smalls House

50

window panes, but here this traditional feature has been transformed into a half useful, half decorative one.

Stone and brick were gradually ousting timber framework. But it continued in use for many smaller houses, particularly those in villages for the poorer people. Of a number that survive at Dorchester, the George Inn is among the most interesting. Thought to have been originally the abbey brewhouse, its transformation into an inn involved the construction of a galleried passage at first floor level along one side of the yard. The plaster covered road front of the inn demonstrates the practical drawbacks of timber framing. Without a protective covering it was liable to become less weatherproof as timbers warped or contracted with age and wattle and daub infilling cracked along the edges. Despite its later coating, the George is evidently a building in a tradition of careful craftsmanship.

This tradition had its limitations. Unlike houses for the gentry and the richer farmer, the timber framed village house may have little regard for balanced design, concentrating for the most part on skilful construction.

33. *Galleried centre section, The George Inn, Dorchester, Oxfordshire*

51

34. *Road front, with a jettied upper floor, George Inn, Dorchester*

The jettied upper floors of the George Inn had several practical advantages, in providing more floor space, in protecting the lower walls from the weather and in giving the framework more stability. This stabilising effect is not immediately apparent because to modern eyes these structures look topheavy. In fact, however, the medieval carpenters had found that the weight of wall on the overhang counteracted the spring in the floor joists, which could be further controlled by a beam taken diagonally from one corner of the overhang and known as a dragonbeam.

Farther down the river the occasional timber framed manor house of the 16th century can be found. Dorney Court near Windsor was built about 1510, altered in the 18th century and then carefully restored in

35. *Dorney Court, c. 1500*

recent times to its original character. The front bears a certain likeness to Ockwells with its hall gables and porch, but instead of a courtyard we find the less enclosed and inward looking L shaped plan, a type increasingly adopted in the 16th and 17th centuries. It was easy to roof and gave a fair amount of space, the less important rooms being relegated to the back wing, on to which could be tacked an outhouse or two.

Greys Court at Rotherfield Greys, not far from Henley, dates from

53

36. Gateway, Dorney Court

54

37. *Grey's Court near Henley, showing 16th century front and 18th century addition*

several different periods. The Tudor house stands within a walled enclosure, the earliest part of which on the east is probably from the time of Walter de Grey, Henry III's Archbishop of York. It was not then more than a manor house and was given by the Archbishop to his brother Robert, from whom descended Lord de Grey, Steward of the Household to Edward III. The King gave him leave to make Greys Court into a castle but this was more a matter of prestige than of serious defence. There is only one large tower, known as the Great Tower, dating from this time, the mid 14th century. The medieval living quarters and outbuildings standing against the enclosure walls fell into decay after Greys Court was forfeited to the Crown at the end of the Wars of the Roses. The present house stands clear of the medieval walls, though inside the enclosure, and was built in the 16th century for the Knollys family, distantly connected with the Tudors through marriage with the Boleyns. This is another case of a house built by a courtier, for Francis Knollys, first cousin to Queen Elizabeth I, became Lord Treasurer of the Royal Household. One might have expected something rather grander for a Lord Treasurer, but more of the medieval buildings were probably still in existence at that time and were only destroyed during the Civil War.

38. The Great Tower, Grey's Court, c. 1350

The house which Francis Knollys had built is partly constructed out of stone from earlier buildings and partly of brick courses interspersed with the rough stonework. But although bricks are regarded as stronger than stone rubble, they are still not trusted for the corners of the house, where there are quoins of carefully dressed stone. Similarly the more decorative parts of the exterior, the window surrounds, the doorways and the moulded edge or coping to the roof parapet and gables are stone carved for the purpose.

The main east front of the house is typically Elizabethan in its symmetry. A doorway is placed neatly in the very centre under a moulding which continues over two flanking windows, one on either side. They fill most of the ground floor under the central of three exactly similar gables, each with a small attic window, and on the first floor may have been a gallery running the length of the front. But in the 18th century the house passed to the Stapleton family, who owned plantations in the West Indies and were able to afford extensive redecorations to the interior, as well as a small new wing. There are consequently not many features surviving from the earlier Tudor interior, or from parts of a medieval building on the site.

The most interesting feature of the interior is the plasterwork. This dates from the middle of the 18th century and is of excellent quality, equalling some of the best in an age of good plasterwork. The finest craftsmen in the first half of the century had been Italians, who came over to England and were employed either singly or more often in partnerships on decorating many great houses. English plasterers learnt from them and by the middle of the century had reached a high standard, being paid considerable sums for their more decorative work. As a rule the joiners were the most highly paid of the various craftsmen, though a good part of the payments they received was for the timber used. After them came the plasterers, whose materials were much cheaper and whose skill was correspondingly more highly remunerated.

The plasterer at Greys Court is thought to have been Thomas Roberts. There is no written evidence to this effect and the attribution is solely on grounds of style. Roberts had worked on Oxford college and university buildings since the 1730s and some of his plasterwork there had been fairly restrained. But he also worked at Oxfordshire country houses, such as Rousham and Ditchley, and the designs at Greys Court certainly show accomplishment and inventiveness, such as one might expect from a versatile and experienced worker.

39. *Drawing Room, Grey's Court, showing Rococo plasterwork*

40. *The Drawing Room, Grey's Court (detail)*

In the Drawing Room there are graceful festoons and vases of fruit and flowers in an easy, flowing manner. Doves with bows and arrows have suggested to one authority a reference to the marriage of Sir Thomas Stapleton in 1765, though by this time the Rococo style of plasterwork was rapidly going out of fashion, having been supplanted by the more severe Neoclassicism of the brothers Adam. A date before 1753 is unlikely because the plaster designs in one room appear to be taken from a book published in that year, *The Ruins of Palmyra* by Robert Wood. If indeed Thomas Roberts is the plasterer at Greys Court, this is an instance of an Oxford craftsman undertaking work in the countryside within a wide radius of his home town.

From then on the history of Greys Court is characteristic of so many country houses. The later Stapletons of the 19th century lacked the taste of their forebears and proceeded to add an incongruous billiard room and bay windows filled with plate glass. Between the wars they sold the house and it passed to an owner who was prepared to do the useful archaeological work of removing the Victorian additions, though it was not put back exactly as before. New Tudor windows were inserted in place of the Victorian bays which in their turn had taken the place of areas of plain walling. A delightful garden in and around the enclosing walls and outbuildings was carefully tended and perfected, a garden essentially, however, of the 20th century, both more consciously informal in its design and more varied in its plants than any Tudor garden.

Many of the smaller Tudor houses have been much altered. One that has been carefully restored to nearly its original condition is the White Hart Inn at Fyfield. It probably started as the dwelling house of a fairly prosperous member of the yeoman class in the 16th century. One might expect this class to have a different type of house from that inhabited by a lord of the manor, but in this case at least, as in many other cases in Tudor times, the yeoman's house is a scaled down version of the manor house. There is a central hall, with a kitchen and service wing at one end and a wing for the owner and his family at the other. The second of these wings is at right angles to the hall and is carried back to give the house a plan in the shape of an L. This is the same type of plan as at Dorney Court.

Of the different parts of the house, the two wings represent innovations during earlier centuries. The free-standing hall of Norman times has given place to a slightly more complex structure in which the hall is the basic element, while the other two elements, the wings, are thought of still as additions. This affects the way in which the three parts of the house are built. More advanced types of construction are used on the

59

wings, more traditional ones on the hall. Even in the hall itself, there have been some changes that become apparent if one compares it with an earlier neighbouring building, Fyfield Manor House. Among the surviving medieval parts of this house is a large room on the first floor which was originally the solar, a retiring room for the lord of the manor and his family. It dates from the 14th century and has a magnificent roof of very heavy timbers. Great tie beams stretch across the room from above the level of the top of the walls and slope up to a central point. The beams are strengthened by solid timbers beneath them on either side, each shaped on the underside into two curves meeting in a sharp point. This pattern is repeated on the wind braces on to which the rafters are fixed, so that the general impression of the roof is that of a series of massive curved and pointed timbers.

The hall roof at the White Hart follows this traditional type of construction with some significant differences. There are the same curved wind braces, the same curving supports under a central beam. But in the

41. *The White Hart, Fyfield, c. 1500*

passage of some two centuries, the art of building timber roofs had been refined and made far less cumbrous. Some, admittedly, of the extra decorative effect has been whittled away in the process, so that the double pointed curves have been replaced by single, unpointed ones. Yet there are a number of gains which come from simplifying the structural forms. By placing the beam higher up it has been possible to make the supporting timber underneath into a single graceful arch. Of the two tiers of wind braces on either side, the upper ones are contrived to give an appearance of further arches.

At one end of the hall there are arched timbers in the framework of the wall. This is the only place where there is an effect of a pointed arch, though interrupted by a post cutting through the apex. The central arch under the beam accords with the Tudor preference for a much more gentle, flatter curve than in earlier, medieval buildings.

One interesting feature of the hall is the large tall window. In a manor house, the part of the hall where the lord of the manor dined was lit by a similar window which in Tudor times and even earlier was often enlarged to form a projecting bay. This fashion was comparatively recent and the owner of what is now the White Hart apparently did not feel the need to adopt it, but even in the much smaller space of his humbler hall he kept the distinction between his own end of it and the so-called lower end for dependants. This is where the two outer doors are placed, one opening on to the street, the other immediately opposite leading to the yard at the back, providing an adequate, and in winter probably an excessive, current of fresh air.

There is no early fireplace in the hall and we can only guess at the method of heating the room. Perhaps it would have had a charcoal brazier, the fumes from which would have escaped through louvres at one end of the roof where there is a triangular wall space. This small section of wall rises above the level of the adjoining roof of the cross wing and provides the most convenient place for introducing ventilation. It had been sealed by weatherboarding before the restoration of the building, in the early 1960s, and has now apparently been cement rendered and given a coating of lime wash.

There is a wide fireplace in the owner's wing beyond the upper end of the hall. This is so large that it has to be spanned by a heavy beam known as a bressummer and the space within is obtained by building out beyond the main wall. The massive stone built chimney stack is gradually diminished as it goes up by stages that are roofed and known as offsets. The final top part is a modern brick shaft which may replace an earlier brick one of approximately the same sort. Another large chimney

stack occupies a corresponding place at the kitchen end of the house. These balancing end stacks are more a matter of practical necessity than of conscious design. The Renaissance idea of strictly symmetrical architecture had scarcely penetrated to the yeoman.

42. *Original House, No. 39, The Causeway, Steventon, Berkshire*

Still smaller houses on more cramped sites dispense altogether with the central hall. Sometimes when a villager in a cruck cottage found himself more prosperous, he would add a wing to the side of his house which would provide him with the same kind of rooms as in the owner's wing at the White Hart. This appears to be what happened to No. 39, The Causeway, Steventon, a house restored not long ago after having been split up into several cottages. The original cruck dwelling faces the road and has a semi circular oven projecting from the main wall at the side, where the cruck timbers are exposed to view above a stone base wall. At the other end of the house a taller cross wing was built some time later perhaps in the 15th or early in the 16th century. This displays an advanced and highly decorative type of timber frame construction, which can best be seen on the gable wall facing the road.

One thing immediately stands out in this wall. The builder is very

43. *North-west gable, No. 39, The Causeway*

sure of his method and of the type of design which he wants to achieve. Each of the main timbers which are exposed free of plaster are essential to the structure and at the same time contribute to a carefully composed, decorative pattern. There is no longer a cautious reliance on the closely set rows of posts which marked the more hesitant type of framework when there was always plenty of wood to spare. A growing shortage of timber may have made the builder more daring. He embarked on wide panels and braced them with crossed diagonal struts, all securely pinned together with wooden pegs so that there was the minimum of movement in the framework. When placing a window in the middle of the first floor, he was careful to prevent bending of the beam above by giving it two extra diagonal struts which at the same time echo the slanting curves of the boards that edge the gable ends.

It has been suggested by one authority that the two wings of this house were built at the same time. Some of the old roof tiles could, it is said, be as old as the 14th or even the 13th century, implying that the roof would have been tiled at that time. Another point in favour of a medieval date for both parts of the house is the fact that the wind braces are the same shape throughout. According to this argument, the cruck wing formed a small medieval hall while the two storey cross wing contained various rooms such as the solar, or retiring room for the owner and his family.

Against this view of a single building date there are one or two points of difficulty. The timbers are admitted to be very slender for so early a period and the design of the taller wing can be shown to resemble houses in the same village which are almost certain to date from the late 16th or early 17th century. Most early roofs which were not of cruck form had either one or two posts going between the beams and the upper part of the roof; here there is none in the middle of the roof. The thin central posts on the gable end are characteristic also of quite late timber framework.

So the reader must be left to judge the evidence. This is one of those cases where there are some telling points to be made for both points of view. They cannot easily be explained away. There is no doubt that the two different types of timber construction could be used side by side and during the same period. On the other hand one can point to the improbability of a very light timber framework at so early a date. This instance has been discussed in detail to show the difficulties which can beset experts in trying to establish even approximate dates for the construction of a single small house.

The builder of No. 39 The Causeway, produced a symmetrical design within the narrow compass of a gable end. Another and more elaborate

44. *No. 127, The Causeway*

instance of this type of design is to be seen at No 127, at the corner of Mill Street. This is another L planned house with a much shorter block facing the road. It is one further step removed from the hall house where the cross wing had still been subordinate to the block containing the hall. Here the wing has taken over as the main part of the house and whereas the hall had once received the most elaborate decoration, this is now lavished on the wing. In addition to the curved patterns of struts, which are more complicated than on No. 39, the main beam of the gable end is brought forward and given a row of bulbous, pointed pendants, one at each end and two in the middle in front of a wide lattice window. Both ground and first floor windows occupy a wider area of the frontage than would have been the case on earlier houses. They now have equal importance with the timber framework as display features, so that where previously the windows appear as openings within the framework, they are here brought forward almost as if they were escaping from the frame to become separate, and as it were autonomous, elements in the composition. How far this whole timber framed architecure had come by the very last years of the 16th and first part of the 17th century can be appreciated if one compares this house with a simpler one, Lyford Grange, where though there have been many alterations, the repetitive pattern of close set timbers can clearly be seen on the back wall.

45. *Lyford Grange, Berkshire*

46. *Manor Farm, Chalgrove, c. 15th–16th century. Note the overhanging upper floor, typical of the period*

Many medieval houses were much altered in the 16th century. As the use of a central hall went out of fashion, householders began to look at the empty space in the upper half of the hall with a view to utilising it for bedrooms, just as spacious lofts are converted into bedrooms at the present day. The insertion of a first floor presented no great difficulties when the outer walls and the roof were already there. A staircase would have been built in one of the wings and openings through at first floor level from rooms or landings were all that was needed once the new floor in the centre had been inserted. With the new windows placed in openings created in the upper walls of the former hall, the house took on the appearance of a two storeyed structure throughout, as well as now being one in fact.

As a result the early origins of these houses are often unrecognised. Sometimes there have been later repairs and alterations which further disguise the character of a former hall house. A case where this has happened is the Manor Farm at Chalgrove. Viewed at a distance from the road, there is hardly any trace of timber framework, the windows and chimneys are mainly Victorian and most of the front wall is covered with a layer of cement. Yet the plan of the house might suggest the possibility of a medieval hall within the central range, while the overhanging first

floors of the gables on either side indicate the likelihood of timber framed construction. Hidden within the central block above later ceilings is a timber roof of the same type as that of the White Hart Inn at Fyfield and dating probably from the 15th century. Various stone fireplaces of 16th century date show that extensive work was done on the house at that time, when the first floor of the central block is likely to have been inserted. The gabled wing on the right has a rather similar roof and is probably as old as the central hall. One significant feature, which can be seen from the road, is the lower roof ridge of this wing, leaving a triangular space at the end of the main roof where there was room for smoke and fumes to escape from the hall. There are unlikely to have been any fireplaces or chimneys in the hall range before the 16th century.

The roofs of even quite large houses continued to be thatched in the 16th century. It was a convenient covering since the material required could be either long straw, wheat reed, bracken, rushes, broom or even heather and the foundation above the rafters need only be wattle on to which the layers of thatch were secured by hazel rods. It was always possible to obtain some suitable material locally and the craft was easily learnt (though the finished result might vary considerably according to

47. Thatched cob wall, west of the Church at Appleford

the skill used). So popular was thatching that it can be found not only on houses but also as a covering for walls that could be damaged by damp. West of the church at Appleford can be seen a long thatched wall which is built of cob, a mixture of chalk and mud with some chopped straw and gravel.

Small thatched houses can be seen in such villages as South Morton and East Hagbourne. The one illustrated shows the characteristic variation in the eaves line, which is taken up round the first floor windows. The timber framework of this house is of a type which had great advantages for the poorer countryman. It used the minimum amount of timber

48. *Thatched house at South Morton*

and was reasonably stable. At the same time the regularity of the spaces between the framework allowed them to be filled with wattle panels that varied in size within a fairly narrow range. A house such as this might originally have contained only one room on the ground floor with a fireplace at one end. A ladder would have led to the first floor, divided into two bedrooms.

69

CHAPTER IV

The Stuart Period

The 17th century in the Thames Valley saw two forms of building. For the smaller houses and those structures of a practical nature, such as barns and mills, traditional methods and styles continued to be employed, while for the larger and grander buildings, whether country houses or town halls, styles began to change in accordance with new fashions spreading from the capital.

An example of the more traditional type of building is the Old Chequers Inn at Clifton Hampden. It embodies whatever materials were to hand and were found suitable. A secure base was provided by stonework, a thick band of which carries round the outer walls and removes the upper timber framework from risk of decay from damp near the ground. Plaster was used for infilling between the timbers and, since this too could suffer decay unless kept fairly dry, the roof was given a thick covering of thatch which spreads out over the eaves to lead rainwater down clear of the outer wall surfaces. The resultant variety of materials, all arrived at by the logic of convenience and appropriateness, provides without any deliberate contrivance a very picturesque and pleasing effect.

A type of building still much in use in this century is the dovecote. It could provide a welcome source of winter food in an age when fodder for cattle was often scarce and is usually to be found near a manor or large farmhouse. The Manor Dovecote at Culham was constructed as late as 1685 to contain no less than four thousand nests in the hollows of bricks specially shaped for this purpose. The outside walling is of rough limestone, quarried locally and edged at the angles base and eaves with bricks for greater neatness and stability. Local craftsmen were finding that bricks could be just as efficient for accurate wall finishes as carefully hewn blocks of stone, though at first they tended to avoid using bricks over openings where there were heavy loads of wall to support. The

49. *Tudor dovecote at Long Wittenham*

Tudor dovecote at Long Wittenham, still in use, is another example.

Roof tiles were also coming into more general use. They lessened the weight which the wall itself had to carry, for the limestone slates were thick, large and heavy. The tiles which cover the roof of the Manor Dovecote needed lighter timbers to carry them than would stone slates and the fact that the tiles gave less insulation from heat and cold was in this case beside the point, however much it might be a drawback for a house roof. The Dovecote at Ascott House, Stadhampton, is also tile covered but the walls are eight sided, brick faced and finished at the eaves in an elegant pattern of small arches reminiscent of carved stonework. As a home for pigeons, this is one of the most decorative in the country and is more than halfway to being an ornamental adjunct to Ascott House, now unfortunately demolished. For technical skill, the Dovecote stands comparison with a building as important in the society of the time as the Town Hall at Watlington, erected in 1664–5.

71

50. *Town Hall, Watlington, c. 1664, showing elaborate brickwork*

Here, as at Ascott House Dovecote, specially shaped bricks were made in moulds. It was a quicker and easier technique, provided that enough of one shape were needed, than the alternative process of cutting the rectangular brick cubes with a special axe to a rough shape which would then have been rubbed smooth with a hard stone. The Town Hall is an exercise in making brickwork follow the same outlines that a mason would have arrived at by carving in stone. A large building all in this

style of brickwork might well become monotonous, but the Town Hall is saved from this defect partly by its small size and partly by its weatherboarded wooden turret capped by a wrought iron weathervane.

The builders of the later 17th century may have been aware of this danger of monotony. It was about this time that they both achieved a more regularly shaped brick, needing only thin mortar joints, and began to experiment with chequered patterns of alternating red and grey bricks. They would also try out the effect of one colour of bricks for the main wall surface and another at the angles and round windows and doors. Shell House at Hedgerley has a typical arrangement of red bricks laid as stretchers, that is with their long sides showing as part of the outer wall surface, and blue grey bricks alternating as headers, with their short sides outermost. The builder punctuated this pattern with two horizontal bands, a brick one at the first floor level and a painted wooden one at the eaves. The central feature which draws the design together is a finely moulded doorhood on beautifully carved brackets.

This subtle type of design was still an exception in the later 17th century. The best architects continued to rely on well carved stonework as a decorative finish for buildings which had to look impressive. The Guild Hall at Windsor is a good example of this sort of building, for the architect had to provide the royal borough with something appropriate to its status as a favourite residence of the monarchy with a newly refurbished royal castle. Small in size, the Guild Hall was given a wide range of fashionable architectural details: arches, columns, cornices, even two statues in arched niches. The design is often attributed to Sir Christopher Wren, who supervised the carrying out of one provided in 1687 by Sir Thomas Fitch. His ornate building gained much from the contrasts of tone, colour and texture which brick and stone provided. The darker red brick, its surface divided into small rectangles and squares by the mortar joints, provides a foil for the lighter, creamy grey stone composed of much larger blocks with their surfaces broken more by the carving than by the fine joints. As one's attention is directed to the skilled workmanship in stone, there is a tendency to think of the whole building in these terms. If all had been brick or all stone, it would have been difficult for the designer to make half his statement, as it were, in italics.

Despite the advantages of a mixture of brick and stone, there was such a strong tradition of stonework in and around Oxford that very few brick structures were built there until much later. This traditionalism affected not only choice of materials but also choice of style. One instance of this is Carfax Conduit. Otho Nicholson, one of the richer Fellows of Christchurch College, paid for it to be built in 1616 as part of a scheme to bring

73

51–52. Above, *north-end and* below, *south-end of Guildhall, Windsor*

fresh water to the city. Wooden pipes conducted water from a spring on Hinksey Hill down as far as the stone tank which formed the lower part of the Conduit. Round the top of this tank runs a pierced parapet formed partly out of the donor's initials, O N which are interspersed with mermaids who are holding combs in one hand and in the other looking glasses. Four stone ribs rise from the tank and curve upwards and inwards like flying buttresses to support a tall eight sided pinnacle. Small statues, once partly gilded, stand in niches round the pinnacle and carved animals decorate the top of the parapet, so that the whole effect is that of an elaborately fanciful structure, an equivalent in stone of the more imaginative literature of the time. Francis Bacon in his essay "Of Gardens" suggested that they should have fountains with "ornaments of images gilt, or of marble" and a bathing pool encompassed "with rails of low statuas", admitting however that fountains "be pretty things to look on, but nothing to health and sweetness". Since he was a Cambridge man, he may not have been aware how Oxford managed to combine ornament with a practical aid to health in bringing sweet water to the city.

An Oxfordshire writer, Anthony A Wood, proudly asserted that "for its images of ancient kings about it, gilding and exquisite carving the like (except probably in London) not to be found in England". The kings are the figures in the niches, eight in all comprising the Biblical King David, Alexander the Great, the Crusader Godfrey of Bouillon, a King of the Goths, Charlemagne, Hector of Troy, Julius Caesar and James I (in whose reign the Conduit was made). On the four ribs or arches are figures of Justice, Temperance, Fortitude and Wisdom. Of these Temperance is pouring wine from a larger to a smaller container and Wisdom holds a snake biting its own tail, an ancient symbol of eternity. The four heraldic animals on the corners of the parapet are an antelope, a dragon, a lion and a unicorn holding the banners of England, Scotland, France and Ireland in front of them. Above the pinnacle is a figure facing in two directions with the head of an old man looking one way and that of a young woman holding a sceptre looking the other way. The total cost of this splendid contrivance was over two thousand pounds, a very large sum in those days for a structure only twelve feet square.

Later in the 18th century it was found that the Conduit obstructed traffic in the centre of Oxford. The university generously and resourcefully gave it to Lord Harcourt to be put up in his park at Nuneham Courtenay, where it had no function other than as an ornament in the carefully landscaped grounds. By contrast the Well Head round the spring on Hinksey Hill, from which the water came, is a much plainer

53. Carfax Conduit, c. 1616, Nuneham Courtenay, Oxfordshire

affair, as befitted a building intended for the countryside. It too is of stone but dates from 1634 and shows a better understanding of the new classicising style, the only ornate carving being a stone cartouche representing the form of a sheet of vellum paper, its edges curling over inwards as though it was partly unrolled.

Most village houses lacked even this amount of carving. What they had was usually closely related to the main structural features such as windows and doorways. Some of this type of carving can be seen on The Bear and Ragged Staff Inn at Cumnor near Oxford, though one has to go round to the back to see any carved stone window heads. The central ground floor window in front and the doorway beside it have wooden lintels over them which are carved in a more intricate manner than most stone ones each having rows of different patterns one above the other within a fairly narrow breadth, since the lintels are rather thin for the weight of wall above them. This has led to the use of stone arches imbedded in the walls above some of the front windows. Although decorative in effect, the purpose of these stone arches is essentially a practical one of taking most of the weight of the wall above and distributing it either side of the arch away from the weakest point, the centre of the window head.

The plan of The Bear and Ragged Staff is a fairly characteristic one. On either side of a recessed central range are two projecting, gabled wings, not unlike the two wings at either end of a medieval hall. But although many houses in the 16th century had central halls rising two storeys in height, the smaller house of the 17th century in the middle Thames Valley generally had two or more floors throughout. This was to lead eventually to a more compact type of house, but here the balancing pair of wings add both variety and a certain formality to offset the rough stonework, or rubble, much of it laid at random without courses. The coursed rubble of the gable on the left of the doorway suggests that this part of the front wall may have become unsafe and needed rebuilding in a stronger manner.

The Inn has two large chimney stacks. They are both to begin with part of the stone structure of the house and it is only at the level of the separate shafts above the massive main stacks that brick is used. Since brick stacks can be rather thinner and neater, the stonework here is some indication of the relative ease with which the local builders acted as masons and of their unfamiliarity with bricklaying. The shafts are characteristic of the early 17th century in being less ornate than most Tudor ones but they are given some decorative quality by bands at the bases and caps and by being set diagonally on top of the stacks. The import-

77

54. Bear and Ragged Staff, Cumnor, note window lintels

ance attached to the main fireplace in houses at this time is shown by carving that runs along the great beam over a fireplace on the ground floor. The space needed for these wide, deep fireplaces was obtained by building out from the main walls of the house, the chimney being still thought of as though it were an addition to something already complete rather than an essential part of a house and built at the same time as the rest of it. People seem only gradually to have realised that a chimney built near the centre of a house instead of on to the outside wall would not only provide fireplaces for rooms on either side but also lose less heat through its walls and so keep the house warmer.

55. *Culham Manor*

Internal chimneys were, of course, by no means unknown in the early 17th century. They are even found within quite early houses which were altered in the 17th century, as for example at Culham Manor. This had once been a grange of Abingdon Abbey and was bought after the disso-

lution of the monastery by a wool merchant named William Bury. His grandson Thomas remodelled the house between 1600 and 1614, providing no more accommodation but a more up to date appearance from outside the main entrance. The abbey grange was probably, to judge from what remains, a serviceable but unpretentious dwelling round three sides of a courtyard. It was soundly constructed with stone walls to the ground floor and timber framework above, but Thomas Bury wanted an impressive stone front to his house and this he obtained by refacing the longest side opposite the parish church. All that survives of this front is a recessed block flanked by two gabled wings.

Thus far the plan resembles that of a village house such as The Bear and Ragged Staff Inn at Cumnor. The left gable, however, contains a dignified, almost stately porch, its lintel head carved with Thomas Bury's initials and the date 1610. From what is known of Jacobean houses in general, it is at once apparent that an important entrance porch would not have been placed to one side of a facade but in the middle, in order to produce a symmetrical design. This supposition is borne out by the strictly balanced arrangement of the porch and the neighbouring windows, one on either side and a larger one above, forming a triangular composition. The Jacobean front of the house would have had three gables, a central one with the porch and two balancing ones at either end joined to the centre by recessed ranges. There would thus have been five main parts to the front, of which three still survive.

The porch is an interesting design. It has some characteristics which go back to Tudor and medieval houses, such as the link between the stone window heads with moulded bands either side and the projecting stonework over the porch itself. The small repetitive stone pattern above the windows occurs again in a smaller, slightly different form in the centre and the two little classical obelisks over the porch are not far removed in shape from Gothic pinnacles. Most of the details of the carving, however, conform to the new Renaissance standards, so that the porch arch is round instead of pointed and the two brackets above are given the correct new scroll form. The design is in effect transitional between old and new.

Another transitional house is Garsington Manor. As the home of Lady Ottoline Morell in the early years of this century, it has become famous for the writers and artists,—Julian and Aldous Huxley, Dora Carrington, Lytton Strachey and others,—whom she gathered there. Its society in those days has been described with some pardonable exaggerations in Aldous Huxley's novel *Crome Yellow*. But the architecture of his country house does not (intentionally) bear much resemblance to Garsington, for

56. *The Manor House, Garsington*

he writes of a brick house with towers standing on a high terrace. The Manor House at Garsington is of stone, without towers and stands on a level site. It dates from the 16th century, when it was occupied by a yeoman farmer, Lawrence Whistler, and was partly remodelled when it came into the possession of the Wickham family in 1625. William Wickham was from Sussex (though his ancestors had lived at Swalcliffe in Oxfordshire) and acquired the property through marriage to a local heiress, Jane Brome.

The Wickhams remained squires until the middle of the 18th century. No alterations were made to the house in the later years of their ownership owing, no doubt, to the fact that the great grandson of the first Wickham owner, another William Wickham, died as a young man in 1727, leaving the house to his widow. After various changes of ownership it was bought by the Oxford lawyer, Philip Morell, in 1914. There were thus only two main periods of building activity, both of which are apparent on the entrance front. Its three gables above stone mullioned windows are characteristically Tudor, while the arched doorway with its stone hood is an addition of the later 17th century. Fortunately the curve of the doorhood echoes that of the window arches on the ground floor, though the detailed carving of the doorway and window arches is very

81

57. *Front doorway, Manor House, Garsington*

different. The keystone beneath the hood, for example, is a strictly classical feature, as are the scroll brackets on which the hood is supported. The moulding which runs along above the windows, on the other hand, is only slightly modified from medieval ones. Yet there is no harsh break in style, for the doorhood and window head mouldings join almost as if they had been designed and built together. The Manor House illustrates the gradualness of changing fashions in the countryside.

The new style only came to fruition in the late 17th century and is represented by another stone building, the impressive Town Hall at Abingdon. This accomplished design, dating from 1677, is of a type that can be traced back to Michelangelo's buildings for the Capitol at Rome. One resemblance lies in the range of tall pilasters (like flattened columns) that, with the pedestals on which they stand, extend to nearly the full height of two lofty storeys. Another similarity is the arrangement of a ground floor left partly open to the public and a first floor that is enclosed in the usual way by walls and windows. Here the likeness ends, for Abingdon's Town Hall has arches to both floors and a steeply pitched English roof with dormer windows. In the centre of the roof above the dormers a wooden parapet encloses a flat central space on which stands an eight sided wooden turret capped by a small dome or cupola.

The masonry is excellent. Its fine joints for the plain blocks and crisp outlines to the carving accord with the highly finished work that Sir Christopher Wren demanded during the rebuilding of the City of London churches after the Great Fire of 1666. Many of his masons came from Oxfordshire and one of them, Christopher Kempster, was the builder and perhaps also the designer of Abingdon Town Hall. He was

58. Town Hall, c. 1677, Abingdon

83

not only a mason builder but as well the owner of a quarry at Burford from which he shipped stone down the Thames in barges. At Abingdon he could provide the stone, the skilled craftsmanship and in addition the fruits of his experience in working for the greatest English architect of his day.

Wren's influence can also be seen in the Upper School at Eton. It faces the road and acts as the fourth side of the great quadrangle which has been described in the chapter on medieval architecture. In materials it resembles the Town Hall at Windsor across the river, being a combination of brick and stonework, and in design it bears a strong likeness to Wren's Library for Trinity College at Cambridge. These similarities have led people to suggest that Wren might himself be the architect of the Upper School. But the building has one or two faults of style of which Wren would not have been guilty at that time. It was begun in 1689 and Wren was by then an experienced architect of many years' standing. He is unlikely to have designed the awkwardly shaped central arch, which looks as if it has been stretched to fit the width of the passageway behind it; nor would he have squashed in the two first floor windows on either side of the central projection when all the other windows have plenty of wall space round them.

59. *Upper School, Eton*

These solecisms suggest a follower of Wren. The obvious choice is Matthew Bankes, the builder employed on the Upper School by the Provost of Eton, John Newborough. Bankes had an official post in the government's Office of Works as Master Carpenter, a position of some responsibility which carried with it an official residence in the Stable Yard of Chelsea Hospital. He had been Wren's surveyor in charge of the construction of Trinity College Library in 1676 and was called in again when the floor of the library needed strengthening some ten years later. So it seems extremely likely that he adapted Wren's design to fit the new building at Eton. This process of adaptation and copying was one of the ways in which the works of great architects were transmuted into the accepted practice of craftsmen builders.

When one comes to the typical details of 17th century architecture in the Thames Valley, the best instances are to be found among the houses of the minor gentry and clergy, neither too grand to have altered their dwellings later at the dictates of fashion nor so humble as to have been unable to afford good workmanship. Such a house is Ipsden Vicarage, built in 1643. It is up to date in using brick for the main walls, which stand on a base of local flints. Its roof of old tiles was made possible by the use of these bricks, since the baking of tiles in those days required a batch of bricks in the kiln to ward off some of the heat and so prevent the tiles from being burnt. But these two materials which provide an external covering had not done away with the old skill and delight in woodwork. Round the roof runs an elaborate wooden bracketed cornice, while the windows retain the original wooden framework with the characteristic shape of a cross inside a rectangle. The four lights thus formed in each rectangle are iron casements. Inside the house in the ground floor rooms are moulded beams and ceiling cornices with small brackets. As in so many houses of the 17th century, much skill and thought was devoted to the woodwork of the staircase, which is of the same date as the main structure and has painted balusters.

Another carefully constructed staircase of the 17th century survives at Lower Grange, Drayton Saint Leonard. It has newel posts at the end of each flight capped by ball finials. These posts, which were a necessary part of the structure, have been made into decorative features in the same way that the handrails between the posts have been given a moulded outline and the balusters turned on the lathe to provide a varied, curving shape. The exterior of Lower Grange is an interesting mixture of work of different periods in the 16th and 17th centuries.

Western House, Marlow, in Western Street, can show more fine workmanship. It dates from 1699 and has walls of chequer brickwork which

60. *Old Vicarage, c. 1643, Ipsden, before reconstruction*

act as a closely patterned backcloth to details in other materials. At the top of the pipes leading down from the roof gutters are beautifully cast lead rainwater heads carrying cherub heads and wings and the initials of the then owner and his wife, ICM, the C placed above the other two letters and standing for the surname, the I (perhaps in place of a J) for the

owner's Christian name and the M for the Christian name of his wife. At the eaves level there is also a neatly carved wooden cornice, but the best woodwork is to be seen round the door, where richly carved brackets on small lion masks support an arched shell hood. Branches, leaves and flowers in high relief twine round the shell, in the centre of which appears another, larger angel head on wings. For a house of moderate size, the quality of work is exceptional and has been unusually well coordinated.

One development in craftsmanship is especially typical of the 17th century. This is the use of fine plaster in various patterns and designs on the outsides of houses, usually those of timber framed construction. The plaster was composed of sand and lime mixed with water and bound together by quantities of finely combed or teased hair from cattle or horses, the ingredients mixed together so thoroughly that they formed a strong, malleable substance which could be spread over a surface without much risk of developing cracks. Light, cheap and durable, especially with a further coating of lime wash, it was an excellent form of protection for the timber framed house. Thin narrow strips or laths of wood were first nailed to the timber framework and these acted as a foundation over and between which the plaster was spread. With a trowel and a rag the face of the plaster could then be worked into designs which might afterwards be picked out in different colours by lime washes. This in essentials is the technique known as pargetting.

Some good examples of pargetting are to be seen at Steventon along the Causeway. One of the best is No. 67, a house dating back to 1657. Its main gable frames the smaller gable of a two storeyed bay with wide casement windows between which runs a band of pargetting decorated in a chequer board pattern. Above the upper window is another triangular area of pargetting with a large fleur de lys picked out in two colours. The result is to give a decorative quality to the bay of a house which is otherwise substantial but not particularly remarkable, the dwelling originally of somebody of middling rank, a yeoman or small merchant below the gentry in status but yet fairly prosperous. Pargetting can be found on smaller houses and is a good indication of the unsophisticated, spontaneous type of ornament of a traditional kind, uninfluenced by the new Renaissance decoration demanded by this time by most of the substantial landowners and by the richer townsmen.

Some pargetting is done by means of a metal comb. This produces fine rows off indentations which can be either straight or curved. The original purpose of this type may have been to deflect moisture from running straight down the walls and forming channels. There are not many examples of this rather more mechanical form of pargetting in the

61. *The Post Office, Appleton, Berkshire*

Thames Valley and it can be somewhat monotonous unless arranged into panels, as on the village Post Office at Appleton where the panels have a rough texture contrasting with smooth recessed borders. These divide the wall into rectangles repeating with variations the rectangular shape of the windows, so that the whole front is formed into an overall pattern. This is broken under the eaves by a small panel where, picked out in colour, are the date of construction of the house, 1690, and the initials of the owner and his wife. Below this the triangular gable of the porch has a remarkably delicate and pleasing pargetted design which is also emphasised by colouring. Its leaves and curling branches remind one of the flowing naturalistic carving on late medieval gables.

Another development in wall covering deserves a brief mention. Tile hanging never achieved in the Thames Valley the popularity which it gained in the south east. The reason for this is probably that timber framework was even more widespread in Surrey, Kent and Sussex, and once a fashion for a particular type of cladding had been established, there were many houses on to which it could be fixed. Tile hanging is certainly not unknown on the timber framed buildings along the Thames. One place where it can be found is East Hagbourne. Some tile hanging there is on a timber framed house of the 17th century and is used only for the triangular upper sections of the gables where most protection was needed from wind and rain. Lower down the walls revert to the usual plaster infilling.

Brick infilling of timber framework occurred frequently during this period. Bricks had become plentiful and could easily replace decayed wattle and daub. One instance of this brick nogging, as it is called, occurs in a very decorative form on a house next to the churchyard at Long Wittenham. Many of the panels are filled with a herringbone pattern of brickwork, contrasting with others in the usual Flemish bond,

62. Brick nogging at Long Wittenham

that is, bricks laid alternately with their long and short sides facing out-wards. The name Flemish bond has got attached to this method of laying bricks for no very good reason, since it is not particularly charac-teristic of Western Belgium.

CHAPTER V

Queen Anne and Georgian Architecture

Abingdon has some excellent houses of the 18th century. In one of them lived the prosperous maltster Benjamin Tomkins, a prominent member of the large Baptist congregation in the town, who left money to found and build the almshouse named after him in Ock Street. In its arrangement the almshouse is very different from earlier ones, having to fit into a long narrow site running back from the road. Two rows of dwellings stretch back on either side of a paved and cobbled pathway which ends in a tall, rather monumental building which is a combination of washhouse and privy. This novel emphasis on cleanliness and hygiene is not allowed to interfere with a somewhat old-fashioned but highly effective architecture. Each row begins on the street front with a fine gable curved in the Dutch manner, the windows picked out in surrounds of different coloured brick and the angles treated as tall pillars capped with great stone balls. Two lower pillars, marking the entrance to the passageway, end in even larger stone pineapples. These gables and pillars frame a vista which ends in the wide arch of the washhouse, its front wall built up to two storeys in height and marked on the upper storey by further pillars framing a long panel and a small but elaborate turret. By contrast the rows of dwellings are treated as single storey, strictly subordinate buildings except half way along each side, where there are small battlemented parapets.

This grandiose project is, of course, far more than an act of practical charity. It expresses a strong sense of civic and probably sectarian pride. Built in 1733, when Nonconformists had only recently achieved a measure of political recognition as subordinate but nonetheless useful supporters of the Hanoverian dynasty, the building asserts something of the importance which rich merchants were beginning to claim. At the same time it is far from being revolutionary and conforms even to outmoded architectural conventions. The curved gables were first introduced to

England in the early 17th century and were not to be seen on any new houses for gentlemen at this time in the middle Thames Valley, however long such forms of building might linger elsewhere.

By the early 18th century an important change of style had occurred. It was only fully and effectively employed on country houses and other buildings for the gentry, where local builders were no longer allowed to use the old traditional forms, such as gables or dripmoulds over windows or flattened pointed arches, however symmetrically these might be arranged. The great national architects, notably Wren, Hawksmoor and Vanbrugh, provided examples by their major commissions in London and in and around Oxford of the new style which lesser architect builders followed down to the smallest details. Kingston House at Kingston Bagpuize is by one of these local men and dates from about 1710–20.

63. Kingston House, Kingston Bagpuize

It was built for the Blandy family, newcomers to the property and eager, it appears, to assert their importance, for stone urns with flames at the corners of the roof are taken from the family arms, which bore three similar urns. The bright red brick walls dressed with stone seem to follow the example set by Wren at Windsor Town Hall and Hampton Court, though the carvings are heavier. In its arrangement of a tall

91

centre and lower wings the house departs from traditional types, the square block plan and the even earlier half H plan round three sides of a courtyard. This new building-up to a monumental centre is emphasised by a bold triangular pediment and by two towering chimneystacks at either side. The house dominates its neighbourhood as confidently as the squirearchy of the time dominated much of the countryside.

Another class of patron is also occasionally found. The new rich were beginning to demand small country houses intended only for short visits and hence without extensive agricultural estates attached. Woodperry near Oxford is one of these houses. It was built for a partner in Child's Bank, John Morse, who had clients in and around Oxford and wanted a fashionable pied-a-terre that would discreetly proclaim his wealth and taste while providing accommodation for himself and a few guests. He chose a local mason, William King, as builder and may have obtained a design from a superior mason-cum-architect, William Townsend, who had built the neighbouring country house of Shotover Park. Woodperry as originally built in 1728–31 cost Morse some £12,000, a large sum in those days for a house with only four bedrooms.

64. Woodperry near Oxford, c. 1720

The reason for this is not readily apparent outside. Admittedly the walls are of finely jointed stone and two arcaded wings curve out round a forecourt entered through intricately wrought iron gates. The ironwork above the gates carries John Morse's monogram in a central oval. But a large part of the cost must have been incurred by the work inside the house, for this was still an age of fine joinery. Much care and labour was expended on delicate wood carvings for the hall and staircase. Behind this central block stand two wings which look original but in fact were added much later in the 1870s.

John Morse's neighbour at Shotover, General Tyrell, had a much larger house. What is of most interest here is not the house itself but a garden pavillion at the far end of a long, canal-like pond. This summer house is one of the earliest examples of the revived Gothic style, using wide pointed arches and battlemented parapets: but there are many things about it which show that this revival was not yet taken seriously. The walls are only faced in cement to resemble stone and the ceiling is vaulted in plaster. The only practical use for the building is as a shelter from which to view the grounds. Its main function is to end the vista from the house and so act as a man-made part of the scenery. This is the beginning of that picturesque approach to architecture which was to become so important later on in the 18th century.

For several decades Gothic was thought fit for park buildings alone. It became an accepted style for setting off the more formal, classical main house; but in the hands of country house builders this revived Gothic took on something of the formal and ornamental qualities of their principal works. The Fishing Lodge at Padworth, now a cottage, shows what happened. It too is battlemented like a castle and cement faced to resemble stone, but its tall window has an elegant pointed arch with a double curve within which wooden bands imitate the intricate tracery of a late Gothic church. This is a Gothic tamed, domesticated and civilised.

A more robust version of this style had been built slightly earlier at Purley. The Hall there, a Jacobean house, was bought in the second decade of the 18th century by a Director of the South Sea Company, Francis Hawes. He employed the great landscape gardener Charles Bridgman to begin laying out a new garden and park with lawns, walks and long avenues. Plants, vases and statues were ordered and Bridgman even planned to transform and enlarge the house into a Venetian villa. But in 1721 the South Sea Company crashed. Francis Hawes was found to have destroyed all evidence of his dealings in Company stock and this suspicious circumstance caused him to be treated with particular severity. All his assets, including the Hall, were confiscated to pay the Com-

pany's debts, leaving him with less than forty pounds as his total capital. Yet when the Hall came to be sold, it was bought back into the family in the name of his younger brother's wife and Francis continued to live there as his brother's guest.

After a decent interval of ten years, work began again with the erection of a pair of lodges and an entrance gateway and on one of the lodges can be seen a brick inscribed with the date 1732, together with the significant initials F H. An even more significant motto appears on a ceiling at the Hall, *Floresco et Evanesco*,—I flourish and vanish. After a further interval of two more decades, the younger brother Thomas gave the ownership of the Hall back to Francis Hawes.

The lodges are ingeniously planned. As each has to look like a miniature tower but is only of one storey, there was space for not more than one room on either side of the gateway. Above this an embattled arch, now unfortunately demolished, provided flues for two chimneys, one from each room. Underneath runs a subterranean passage which connects the rooms and makes the two lodges into one dwelling. Bands of brick and flintwork give a strong horizontal effect to the walls and are continued on the gate piers. Curving side walls flanking the lodges end in massive pillars capped by pinnacles which are more than halfway to being classical obelisks. The circular windows, one now bricked up, are also only half Gothic. There is an uncertainty about the design which suggests that the distinction between Gothic and classical was getting blurred.

By the 1760s the two strands had become interwoven. Bradfield Hall, dating from 1763, combines classical and Gothic features in a way which suggests that the architect saw nothing odd in placing a Doric porch beside windows with pointed arched tracery. This, indeed, is not so much Gothic within a classical framework as an informal placing together of assorted ornaments, such as urns at the roof corners and a triangular pediment that appears for no very obvious reason above an expanse of plain brick walling. An irregular plan with wings of different heights completes an effect of informality very different from the strict symmetry of earlier country houses.

Lower down the Thames Valley nearer Windsor another change was taking place. Unlike the early Stuarts, who preferred to live at Whitehall and to visit Theobalds in Hertfordshire or Greenwich, the later Stuarts, starting with Charles II, made increasing use of their residences in the Thames Valley west of London. The Hanoverians favoured Kew and Windsor, spending so much of their time there that many courtiers and noblemen found it convenient to build houses in the vicinity.

65. Bradfield Hall, c. 1763

One of the earlier of these riverside houses was Marlow Place, dating from 1720 and built for John Wallop, later Earl of Portsmouth, whose considerable estates were some distance away in Hampshire. Yet the house, though of moderate size, is built as a permanent home, perhaps as much by reason of its pleasant surroundings as for its accessability to Windsor and London. Its design is very much in the grand manner, for the architect, Thomas Archer, had studied in Rome, where he may have worked for the great Italian architect of the late Baroque, Carlo Fontana. Not surprisingly, the house recalls Roman villas in its monumental proportions. Its ground floor was intended to house the servants, not yet relegated to a separate wing, as in many later country houses, nor sent underground into basements, but all the same kept 'below stairs'. The first floor was approached by outside stairways, avoiding the need to go through the kitchen quarters, and formed the main living space for the owner, his wife and guests. An upper floor provided bedrooms for children and maidservants.

This social gradation shows clearly outside. The first floor windows are much taller than any others and the two main doorways are given wide stone surrounds. One feature in particular, the design of the stone

95

66. *Marlow Place, c. 1720*

capitals to the great brick pilasters, gives away the Roman training of
Thomas Archer. These capitals, with their scrolls curving inwards, are
taken directly from Roman Baroque buildings, notably those of Fran-
cesco Borromini. Where Archer compromises with English taste is in his
use of brickwork. The Italians of his time preferred stone as more
impressive, and so did most English architects for the more important
buildings of the 18th century. But Marlow Place still betrays the
influence in this respect of Wren's liking for red brick and his brilliant
use of it at Hampton Court not so many years previously.

Another nobleman attracted to the Thames near Windsor was

67. *Monkey Island Hotel, Bray, before reconstruction*

Charles Spenser, third Duke of Marlborough. He had an estate at Whiteknights outside Reading and bought for himself at Bray an island which had once belonged to Burnham Abbey and was known as Monk's Eyot. Here he had built two small summer houses, one called the Pavilion, the other the Fishing Lodge, now enlarged and much modernised to form Monkey Island Hotel. The change from monks to monkeys is linked with the decoration of the entrance hall by Jean-Francois Clermont, whom Horace Walpole described as follows: "Clermont, a Frenchman, was many years in England, painted in grotesque, foliages with birds and monkeys, and executed several ceilings and ornaments of buildings in gardens; particularly a gallery for Frederic prince of Wales at Kew; two temples in the duke of Marlborough's island near Windsor, called from his grotesques, Monkey-island . . ." Horace Walpole adds that "Clermont returned to his own country in 1754."

The paintings are indeed worth noting. Arranged in panels round the ceiling, they form an engagingly frivolous series which shows monkeys fishing, shooting water fowl, riding dolphins, looking at a whale and so on. They contrast with the lodge's sedate exterior which was originally entirely covered in deep chanelling to simulate heavy stonework. Some of this can still be seen. The surface is in fact composed of wooden blocks,

68. *The ceiling, The Monkey Room, Monkey Island Hotel*

the edges cut diagonally, or chamfered, and each block then nailed onto a wooden framework before the whole surface was painted. This elaborate deception needs explaining. It would have been less trouble to have built in brick, by that time the commonest material in this part of the Thames Valley where good building stone had to be brought from afar, and the expense of bricks would not have been great, for the government only started taxing them in 1784. But from being the exception, good brickwork had become the rule, and since many people could afford it, there was no social distinction to be gained from its use. Hence stonework and even anything purporting to be of stone was preferred by anybody claiming superior status. This claim was one of the few which the third Duke of Marlborough could make, for although a competent brigade commander at Dettingen, he had none of his grandfather's brilliance. But it is an indication of the internationalism of the time that a man who spent much of his life fighting the French should have had no objection to employing a French artist to decorate his Fishing Lodge.

In the later 18th century a new source of wealth became available for country house building. The Indian Nabob returned home to establish himself as a member of the landed gentry, spending lavishly in the process. At Basildon Park Francis Sykes commissioned from a fellow York-

69. *Lodge, Basildon Park*

shireman, John Carr, a house as magnificent as any private residence in the county. Rather conservative in style, Carr by-passes the mid-century vogue for mingling Gothic and classical, preferring to keep the two separate. His house is formal, his south east Lodge a picturesque design relying partly on rough flintwork bands for effect, partly on placing a battlemented tower to one side. In using flintwork he may be trying to suggest a primitive, ancient structure that had to be constructed of local materials. He fails to convince because, in an attempt to evoke a sense of the past, he forgot or ignored archaeological accuracy.

Early flintwork was used in the knowledge that it was not particularly strong. The irregular shapes of rough flints meant that a great deal of mortar had to be employed with them and wherever possible a more easily squared material, either stone or brick, held together the corners of walls, where strength was particularly important, or enclosed windows and doorways which needed a regular outline into which wooden frames could be readily fitted. Carr, however, takes flintwork bands right round the eight angles of the Lodge's tower and links them to the windows in the form of keyblocks, as though these would strengthen the arches at their weakest points. We realise, of course, that they do nothing of the sort and are essentially a decorative facing. The main

99

weight of the tower is taken by an inner skin of brickwork.

During the 18th century the Thames was spanned by many new bridges. They were built by men who had to be both architects and engineers, keeping their innovations in engineering within the limits of what was acceptable in appearance, for this was fortunately regarded as of at least equal importance to stability. One or two architects came to specialise in bridge building, among them John Gwynn of Shrewsbury, who designed Magdalen Bridge at Oxford. He was a notable character of the time, a friend of Dr. Johnson, who wrote a dedication to George III at the front of Gwynn's pamphlet *London and Westminster Improved*, a remarkable early essay in town planning. It was a pupil and assistant of Gwynn, William Hayward, who was called on to design a bridge for Henley in place of one which had become ruinous. His design dates from 1781, but he never saw the work started for soon afterwards he caught a fatal feverish cold as a result of giving up an inside place on a coach to a lady.

The rebuilding was sponsored by an important local resident, General Conway, contemporary and friend of that arbiter of taste Horace Walpole, to whom he was related. His daughter Anne was for a short time sent to live at Walpole's Twickenham house while Conway went to Ireland and she received much encouragement and praise from Walpole when later on she became a sculptress. When two keystone heads were needed for the central arch of the new bridge, she was naturally the person chosen to carve them. The one facing downstream is said to represent the river Thame, or Tamesis, and that facing upstream the river Isis. In Egyptian mythology Isis was the wife of Osiris, but Isis is also the name sometimes given to the Thames at Oxford. So if the tradition about the keystones is correct, this is probably one of Walpole's ideas, the two river deities symbolising the marriage of the Thame and the Thames or Isis.

Henley Bridge is built of the deep cream coloured stone which comes from Headington outside Oxford. The design is more unified than that of medieval bridges, which very often have triangular shaped cutwaters rising to the level of the roadway and parapets, so that there is a jagged effect not unlike that of medieval and Tudor roof gables, but in the case of bridges placed horizontally with the pointed ends projecting towards the water. At Henley, William Hayward arranges cutwaters only at water level and slightly above, the tops stepped back to the main wall surface. One is now so used to this form of bridge that it needs an effort to think of it as an innovation, but in effect what has happened is that piers and arches are no longer thought of and expressed as two separate components, they are unified by treating the bridge as though it were a

building pierced by an arcade. The origin of this type of bridge is to be found in Italy and especially in the designs of Alberti and Palladio, whose illustrated writings on architecture had been translated into English, notably by the Venetian architect Leoni, who came to England and worked in the Thames Valley at Cliveden in the 18th century.

There are one or two differences between Henley Bridge and its Italian prototypes. The road surface and the balustraded parapets at Henley are gently curved, sloping up from either side towards the centre, whereas those illustrated and described by Alberti and Palladio have either flat roadways or ones which are flat over the central span and inclined down at an angle either end, a much less graceful arrangement. The Italians preferred their arches semicircular, at least on the more important bridges, and if there were five arches to a bridge they kept the three central ones the same width. But Hayward, because his roadway slopes down from above the central arch, had to make his side arches, of which there are altogether four, lower and so, of a narrower span if they were to be of the same shape as the central arch. He chose arches which are less than semicircles, probably for the practical reason that they give a wider span in relation to their height, and these gentle curves have the added advantage that they go better with the slope of the parapet. Henley Bridge is thus both a sound practical structure and a harmonious work of art, the result of an intelligent patron employing a well trained and skilful specialist in bridge building.

Nuneham Park, another stone structure, is very much the creation of its owners. The old Oxfordshire family of the Harcourts, who had lived not far distant at Stanton Harcourt since the 12th century, acquiring titles and wealth in the 18th, devoted much of their energies to forming a suitable new country residence. The first Earl Harcourt, a cultivated but conventionally minded man, was intent on following accepted rules of taste, one of which was the importance of a good site for one's house with a wide and varied view. He accordingly prepared grounds sloping down to a bend of the Thames by removing the village of Nuneham to a new site a mile away. His recent companion on a tour of Europe, the poet and dramatist William Whitehead, chose the precise place within the park where the house should stand and a competent local architect, Leadbetter, provided a design for it in the approved style of a Venetian villa. A much more talented architect, James 'Athenian' Stuart, was called in to decorate the main room with a splendid coffered ceiling, while for the design of its marble chimneypiece the Earl went to yet another source, the artist Paul Sandby.

The Harcourts found that a taste for building, once acquired, was dif-

ficult to restrain. Lady Harcourt judged the accommodation quite inadequate and persuaded her husband to order two additional wings which had to be joined to the main house by triangular rooms. The house had been begun in 1756 but it was not until the 1760's that the wings as well as the central block were finished. Even so the second Earl, succeeding his father in 1777, was not content to leave the house as it was but immediately set about alterations and improvements, calling in Lancelot 'Capability' Brown to replant the park and Henry Holland to modify and further enlarge the house. Yet more changes occurred in the 1830s when Archbishop Harcourt had the east front of the house remodelled by Robert Smirke, architect of the British Museum, and garden terraces formed by William Gilpin.

The final result of this cumulative process is a grand if slightly formless house in a fine setting. It shows not only the taste and devotion to a civilized country life of an aristocratic family but also the hazards of grafting new styles on old buildings which already have a distinctive character. Fortunately the architects concentrated on good proportions and fairly plain stonework, keeping the richer decoration in marble, plaster and ironwork for inside. Exposing these materials to the damp

70. Nuneham Park, c. 1760

71. Staircase at Nuneham Park

winter atmosphere near the river would have been structurally inadvisable. There was also a strong interest in landscape in the later 18th and early 19th centuries and an appreciation of the soft colours of the English countryside. The brightly coloured exteriors which were acceptable in towns would have been thought garish in the country. The poet William Mason praised the "sweet, gloomy shrubbery" which the second Earl Harcourt planted near the house.

Stone was not the only material allowed for exteriors. As architects and their patrons in later Georgian times became preoccupied with producing buildings resembling those of ancient Greece, so they looked round for some alternative to red brickwork without involving themselves in too much expense. Unfortunately for them, the Thames Valley did not have the right clay for making the pale yellow and grey bricks of East Anglia and the Fenlands, bricks which were thought to harmonise better with stonework from being nearer it in colour. But they could and did use instead the fine, hard plaster which we know as stucco in order to imitate stone. It was easily moulded before setting, so as to resemble stone carving, and the smooth wall surfaces in stucco were lightly channelled to represent the joints between stone blocks. The London Road Lodge at Nuneham shows that by the time it was built, in the early 1830's, country builders were becoming expert in the use of this fairly new material. It had started to be widely used in London in the 1770's after the invention by Liardet of his patented cement. He was followed by a number of other inventors in the next few decades, notably Parker, whose Roman Cement was manufactured at Harwich. Joseph

72. *London Road Lodge, Nuneham Park, c. 1830*

Aspdin's Portland cement, invented in 1824, was more easily obtainable throughout southern England and was also much the strongest of these new products.

Many houses continued to be built of brick and combinations of brick and stone. Builders became adept at devising variations in patterns of the different materials. At Benson one can see two alternatives side by side. The Round House next to the Castle Inn is faced with an arrangement of red bricks combined with the slightly shiny, vitreous bricks, so called from having been baked at a higher temperature in order to produce a hard glazed surface. Wood stoked kilns with plenty of potash in the fumes were the best for this kind of brick. The ends of the bricks were placed in the kiln facing inwards and it is these ends which are laid facing outwards on the wall of the house. As the ends are known as headers when laid in this fashion, the vitreous brickwork on the house is in header bond.

The vitreous bricks form a background, the red emphasise the features of the house. These include not only the windows but also the bands at floor levels. Originally these bands had a structural purpose, projecting out to allow sufficient foothold for the floor joists to rest on the wall beneath. When set nearly flush with the rest of the wall, the bands might

be thought to become no more than a decoration, but they still in this instance have a practical purpose. If these courses of brickwork had been in headers, there would have been little resting place for the joists unless the wall had been of considerable thickness. Built of stretchers, that is with bricks laid lengthways along the outer surface, the bands allow space behind them wherever needed.

The Castle Inn beyond is probably a reconstruction of an earlier building. Benson was on the coaching route from London to Oxford and the Cotswolds and this would have provided both the incentive and the resources for a new inn, taking stone which may have come from the site and using it as a foil to brickwork round the windows. But the main decorative effort is concentrated on the painted woodwork of the doorway and the elaborate scrolls in cast iron round the inn sign.

73. *The Castle Inn, Benson, Oxfordshire*

Another variation on this theme of different walling materials can be seen on a house at Shillingford. Vitreous bricks form a background on the front wall to details picked out in red, while the side wall is built of coursed squared rubble, that is, small blocks of stone of different sizes laid to horizontal courses. Apart from its porch, which is of a much later date, this house relies on contrasts of colour and texture for its effect.

74. *Glazed header brickwork, Shillingford, Oxfordshire*

The projecting first floor band has been dispensed with, probably by means of running the joists parallel with the front and resting them within the thicker stone side walls. The subtlety and restraint of this type of house was sometimes felt to be excessive. Earlier houses no larger had more robust features. One house of the early 18th century in Milton Road, Sutton Courtenay, has a typical fine wooden door surround of the period. Here the contrasts of colour were deliberately bolder, between the white painted woodwork and the red bricks. But what strikes one as

75. *No. 53, Milton Road, Sutton Courtenay, c. 1700*

76. *No. 76, Milton Road, Sutton Courtenay, c. 1600*

an even more important difference in these two houses, typifying the difference between the earlier 18th century architecture and the later, is the decrease in sculptural content. The doorway and window bays at Sutton Courtenay have strongly projecting mouldings which stand out sharply in bright sunlight. The later type of house tends to lack depth.

By the end of the 18th century the smaller house had lost most of its carved or moulded external woodwork. But lack of ornament was not to be tolerated for long. There was a change, as it were, of direction. Instead of going back to the sculptural architecture of the first half of the century, with its projecting bands of brickwork and its rather heavy joinery, the houses remain just as pictorial and add a quality which can only be described as literary. Another house in Sutton Courtenay, No. 76 Milton Road, can explain this trend. Here is a building of a much earlier date, probably the end of the 16th or beginning of the 17th century, which was given new windows at some time around 1800. Instead of providing up-to-date sash windows in serried ranks the builder inserted an assortment of pointed arched casements which make one suspect that the owner had been reading some 'Gothick' novels. They are hardly more implausible and fantastic than the house in its altered state.

CHAPTER VI
Late Georgian and Victorian Period

Windsor Castle is perhaps the most important building in the middle Thames Valley. It is the largest castle in England and has long been a royal residence, but what makes it of great interest architecturally is the way in which work of many periods has been combined into one highly effective composition. Chief credit for this must go to that underrated architect Sir Jeffry Wyatville and his royal patron George IV, who transformed the castle inside and out in the years after 1820.

The task that faced them was daunting enough. Assorted buildings followed a ground plan dating from before Domesday Book (1086) and covering altogether about thirteen acres divided into three enclosures, the upper, central and lower wards. Some of Henry II's stone curtain walls, his square towers at intervals along them, and his central Round Tower survived. Two later kings, Henry III and Edward III, had rebuilt and strengthened the defences, adding circular towers less vulnerable to attack since there were no corner stones to dislodge. Edward's founding of a collegiate church and the Order of the Garter led in the late Middle Ages to the building of the magnificent Chapel of Saint George with quarters for attendant clergy and knights. Henry VIII had added a massive new gateway and Elizabeth I the North Terrace. Then in the reign of Charles II the upper ward gained a set of royal appartments, incorporating various medieval walls and rooms but in a totally different style, as plain outside as they were ornate within. Eventually in the reign of George III an attempt was made by Sir Jeffry's uncle James Wyatt to repair and harmonise a small part of this extraordinary muddle.

George IV's ambition was much greater. It was nothing less than to remodel, by extensive rebuilding, over half the castle,—excluding the chapels and their subsidiary dwellings,—and this was to be done, externally at least, in the Gothic style as it was then understood. There is little point in judging Wyatville's work by later standards, in looking for subt-

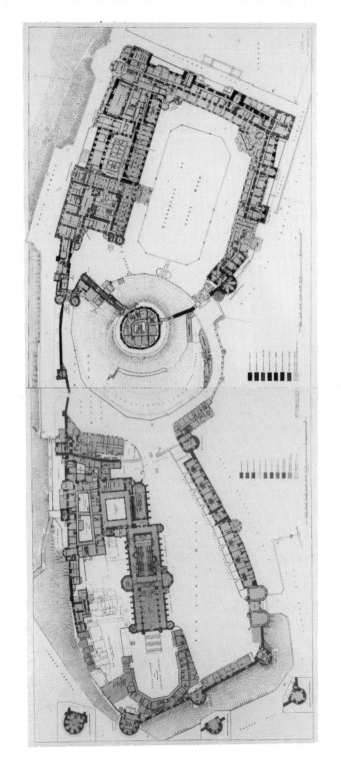

77. *Ground plan of Windsor Castle*

78. *Windsor Castle showing Garter Hall Tower, Henry III Tower, Round Tower,*
Edward III Tower and Lancaster Tower

leties of surface texture, or for the finer distinctions between different periods of Gothic architecture. This is architect's architecture only to the extent that from outside the walls there is a splendid variety of skyline and of different features: towers and turrets, narrow lancet windows and wide battlemented bay windows of many lights, walls alternately recessed and brought forward. Wyatville also knew how to unify this variety. Having heightened much of the upper ward and so obscured the Round Tower, this too was heightened by over thirty feet to provide a central focus. Another instance of his skill can be seen in the so-called Norman Tower, which had in fact been built in about 1360 for Edward III. Here only the gateway and the inner tower are medieval, the outer tower on the left being added by Wyatville to make an impressive, balanced composition.

In effect he restored the castle not to what it was but to what he thought it ought to have been. It became the visual equivalent, in stones and mortar, of the novels of Sir Walter Scott, a romantic evocation of the age of chivalry. Viewed from a distance, the castle took on another, complementary character as romantic scenery, which could be read either in literary terms or as landscape painting made real. This way of looking at architecture may be alien to us today but it is the only way to

understand how Windsor Castle came to acquire its present outward appearance.

The internal alterations to the castle are a different story. Wyatville could not be sure when he started how much of the structure was sound and could be kept, how much would have to be replaced. To create a sequence of State Apartments he had to work round and above rooms

79. *Windsor Castle showing the Devil's Tower and the Motte Garden*

that were either medieval or from the reign of Charles II. He kept what is now called the Grand Entrance Hall, built in the 1360's for Edward III as an undercroft, a room below a hall. Stone vaulted with pillars running along the centre, it closely resembles a church crypt. Wyatville used similar arches for his adjoining staircase, altered into the Grand Vestibule after another Grand Staircase was built alongside in the 1860's. He also created a splendid late Gothic Guard Chamber, lit by three tall windows under a rib vaulted ceiling which is a much simpler version in plaster of the vault in Saint George's Chapel. It keeps the three lines of ribs along the centre of the ceiling, omitting the star pattern in the Chapel, and achieves an orderly, dignified effect appropriate to the room's purpose.

His Saint George's Hall is less successful. A similar vault is repeated over its unbroken length of a hundred and eighty-five feet. It was doubly unfortunate that in making room for this hall, Wyatville destroyed some remarkable work from the time of Charles II. But elsewhere he was able to retain three rooms which give some idea what this work was like, since they were by the same architect, Hugh May. For the Queen's Audience Chamber, the King's Dining room and the Queen's Presence Chamber, all dating from the 1670's, May commissioned ceiling paintings from the Italian Antonio Verrio, while Grinling Gibbons and Henry Phillips were employed to ornament the walls with festoons carved in wood. These carvings, varied in the Dining room to include game and shellfish, show an extraordinary skill unequalled in Europe. Verrio's ceilings are less accomplished but the idea behind them is interesting because seldom put into practice in England. Above painted borders they represent the open sky, peopled with figures on clouds or flying through the air. This type of painting has by now become so familiar as to be viewed, if not with contempt, at least often with indifference. But at the time, Verrio's work was a daring innovation for this country, only heralded by the Banqueting Hall ceiling in Whitehall for Charles I.

Where he could, Wyatville kept the fine ceiling cornices carved by Gibbons and Phillips, in the Picture Gallery, the Van Dyck Room or Queen's Ballroom and the Rubens Room or King's Drawing room. These, with the State Bedroom, have richly decorated ceilings of the 1820's and 1830's, divided after the 18th century manner into panels of different shapes by broad bands with gilded ornament, an occasional small panel or shield being picked out in colour. Combined with damask wall hangings, marble chimneypieces and crystal chandeliers, the effect would be one of great splendour even without the collection of pictures and furniture which these rooms contain.

For still greater opulence, the Grand Reception Room is in a class of its own. In his search for a style which would outshine the florid Neoclassical that had already become too commonplace, George IV harked back to an age where he might well have felt at home, that of Louis XV and Madame de Pompadour. He bought Gobelins tapestry for the walls, French furniture covered in Beauvais tapestry, even busts of Frenchmen of the old regime to set round the room. With its gilt decoration outlining panels on both the walls and the high ceiling, the room is a rather more than lifesize version of the French Rococo style, which, in origin at least, aimed simply at lightness and informality. The result is nevertheless extremely festive. Taken with the earlier rooms decorated by Verrio, it shows the important part played by the English monarchy in introducing artistic styles from abroad. Just as Verrio was employed to decorate country houses as well as royal palaces, so the revived Rococo decoration is to be found in the houses of George IV's closest adherents,—in the Duke of York's house in London, now Lancaster House, in the Duke of Rutland's Belvoir Castle, in Lord Londonderry's Wynyard Park.

Wyatville's last undertaking for George IV was the Waterloo Chamber. It was planned partly as a hall in which to hold an annual banquet in commemoration of the battle of Waterloo, partly as a picture gallery for portraits of sovereigns, statesmen and generals who had contributed to the overthrow of Napoleon and to the subsequent peace settlement. Top lighting was desirable for the paintings and this Wyatville obtained by roofing over a courtyard and providing a roof at two levels, the centre higher than the sides, with a range of windows between them. Round the pictures are further wood carvings by Grinling Gibbons and Henry Phillips. The King died before work could get under way and it was left to his successor, William IV, to order its completion.

The main work of restoration was now complete. It only remained for Queen Victoria and Prince Albert to order a few comparatively minor works, though some were large enough by the standards of ordinary houses. These works were undertaken in a rather different spirit from that which caused Wyatville to design his castellated scenery and his plaster vaults. The new approach was more serious and often more scholarly, as befitted the Victorian age. It was begun by Edward Blore, who was appointed Special Architect to William IV and afterwards to Queen Victoria. He was the son of an antiquary and for many years had acted as an illustrator of books on old houses, castles, churches and cathedrals. He had written and illustrated a book with the sonorous title of *The Monumental Remains of Noble and Eminent Persons*, had been architect to Sir

Walter Scott at his country house of Abbotsford and had designed a complete new 'medieval' country house on the Wye called Goodrich Court. He was thus clearly well fitted to work at Windsor Castle, having proved his adaptability by completing Buckingham Palace in a version of the Neoclassical style. His principal work at Windsor is the Royal Mews, a vast structure with stone walls in the Gothic style, its long, low outline acting as a foil to the tall towers and gateways on the south front of the Castle.

The Mews were completed in 1842 and no more work of importance took place at the Castle until the 1860s. This decade saw the high water mark of the Gothic Revival movement in England as in France. The French Emperor had been received at Windsor by the Queen and Prince Albert and, as a special act of friendship, admitted a knight of the Order of the Garter. The Emperor patronised in France an architect, Viollet-le-Duc, who was perhaps the most influential of all the Gothic Revival architects on the continent. It was natural that the new royal architect at Windsor, Anthony Salvin, should turn to French Gothic architecture when he restored the Curfew Tower, sometimes known as the Clewer Tower, overlooking the road that winds up from the river. Salvin, the son of a general, was a specialist in medieval military structures and had restored many English castles. But he was not lacking in versatility and would if required design in a wide range of styles. For him, as for Blore, the client, and perhaps especially a royal client, was always right.

The Curfew Tower is rounded towards the town. Salvin's tall, steeply pitched roof, following this curve round and ending on the inner face in a sharp gable, is typical of French castles of the 13th century. It is perhaps no accident that Viollet-le-Duc illustrates just such towers and roofs in his famous dictionary of French medieval architecture, written about this time.

Another and slightly later work by Salvin is the Grand Staircase. This too is in a Gothic style of the 13th century, with tall pointed arches and an eight sided roof light of lantern form. Apart from the lantern, which is derived from medieval cathedral architecture, this is really a Renaissance or Baroque type of monumental stairway with a gradual ascent broken by landings. The Gothic forms are only a disguise clothing a plan that is much more expansive than any medieval stairs were given. The nearest approach in England is the great staircase at Christchurch College, Oxford, and this, though Gothic in style, dates from the 16th century.

The last important work at Windsor Castle was by Sir George Gilbert Scott. Like Blore and Salvin before him, he was already a well estab-

80. *Windsor Castle, Curfew Tower*

116

lished architect by the time he came to Windsor and had proved his capacity for designing Gothic buildings as well as his compliance, if need be, in using other styles. But unlike his predecessors, he treated Gothic architecture almost as a matter of faith and had only built the new Foreign Office in the Renaissance style under protest. At Windsor he was only asked to restore the late medieval Horseshoe Court facing Saint George's Chapel. It was not quite to his taste, which was for earlier Gothic, but he achieved a picturesque restoration which reminds one of the growing popularity of half-timbered Tudor buildings in late Victorian England.

If the mark of a good architect is to respond creatively to current fashions, then Scott's design is certainly successful. A covered arcade of carved wooden arches extends in front of the ground floor of the twenty-two houses which had been built in the later 15th century for clergy belonging to Saint George's Chapel. The first floor has exposed wooden framework with many curving timbers and the low pitched roof is edged with a wooden parapet. This is of unusual design because although its outline is battlemented, the battlements are pierced with delicate carving to produce a traceried effect. All three elements of arcade, framework and parapet echo the curving shape to which the building owes its name of Horseshoe Courts.

Windsor Castle shows many facets of the Gothic Revival. The expenditure on it and its subsidiary buildings from the 1820's to the 1860's was enormous and well beyond the purse of any subject. Yet many an English nobleman could afford impressive Gothic battlements if he was content to clothe them in the useful new invention of hard stucco.

The Earls of Macclesfield recast their 14th century castle at Shirburn in stucco in the last years of the 18th century, gradually removing the neighbouring village houses and forming a landscaped park round it which now effectively hides it from public view. Lodges were added, one of them in 1805 by John Nash, already the favourite architect of the Prince of Wales. This favour was due, his enemies said, to the fact that Nash had married a young woman closely connected with the Prince. Yet he was quite as able a practitioner in picturesque Gothic architecture as Wyattville, as his lodge at Shirburn shows. Its narrow lancet windows and the chimneys peeping up behind the battlements show also some of the practical difficulties of designing consistently in this style.

After George IV no British monarch and no small group of wealthy subjects could dictate an architectural style which the rest of the country was content to follow. Just as two parties came to dominate politics, so two main styles, Gothic and Classical, with many variations in each

117

81. *Lodge at Shirburn Castle, c. 1800*

case, tended to divide English architects into opposing camps. This division can be seen in the Thames Valley but for some reason, perhaps the mellowing atmospere of the wooded countryside, there are few of the sharp contrasts in architecture of the period to be found elsewhere. No great Neoclassical mansion in imitation of Greek temples is set down by the Thames, nor, apart from Windsor Castle, are its banks crowned by wildly romantic fortresses such as sprang up in Wales and northern England.

Those country house builders who disliked the Italianate classicism favoured by the great Whig nobles, preferred to imitate Tudor or Jacobean architecture. Disraeli's Tudor Hughenden is just outside the area covered by this book, but an example of this style can be seen at Wallingford. Tudor houses offered not only battlements but picturesque bays and, a practical consideration, wide windows, the best in fact of both worlds.

All the same, there were certain difficulties. The revived Gothic style posed a challenge. It was undeniably dramatic, not only by reason of its association with romantic writings about the Middle Ages but also because it had jagged outlines, deep recesses, bold masses. When Sir

82. Tudor style house built mid-19th century

Francis Sykes of Basildon Park called in John Buonarotti Papworth in 1839 to design new lodges and gates, he required something in the classical style that would yet have more interest than the bland exterior of his 18th century house. Papworth was as good as his middle name and within an ordered Neoclassical scheme provided strong contrasts between voids and solids, smooth surfaces and carved ones. From massive pillars at either end, quadrant railings curve back to meet the finely jointed, smooth stone walls of the lodges. This stonework continues round octagonal turrets, pierced only by tall single windows up to just below eaves level, where a sequence of richly carved panels suddenly breaks the surface. Between the two turrets come three iron gates, the central one flanked by deeply channelled pillars capped by ornate vases which are encircled by cherubs and surmounted by an extraordinary wealth of fruit piled high in pyramids. The whole composition achieves formality without the least monotony.

The Neoclassical style was excellent in the hands of an exceptional architect. When used on the ordinary village house or inn it still manages to achieve elegance. The White Hart at Benson shows what could be done with stucco and metalwork on what is probably a building of the

83. The White Hart, Benson, Oxfordshire

18th century. Brightly painted walls and ingenious ironwork designs on the porch combine to give a sense of cheerfulness. Even more than stucco Gothic, which at least aims at an effect of depth, this is architecture in two dimensions. It was the apparent lack of solidity in stucco houses of this kind that repelled the Gothic Revival architects, quite apart from any hint of frivolity or lack of deeper meaning. To convey depth, seriousness and solidity required a totally different architecture, one which is to be found at Bradfield College, a public school dating from the middle and later years of the 19th century.

The College is of great interest as a complex work of the Gothic Revival. The circumstances in which it was built tell one a good deal about the type of person involved in the movemement and about its aims. As is so often the case when institutions are founded, the architect had to deal with a man of strong character with very definite ideas about what he wanted. In this instance the founder, the Reverend Thomas Stevens, had also a well established social position, being both Rector of the parish of Bradfield and a landowner in the neighbourhood of some generations' standing. He started in the 1840s with the idea of turning his church into something like a small cathedral. But as since the Reformation it was no longer possible to create collegiate churches with a number of canons attached to them, Stevens conceived the notion of forming a choir like those provided by the choral scolars of Magdalen and New College at Oxford. In order to do this, he founded in 1850 a College of Saint Andrew at Bradfield which would give an adequate education combined with special facilities for instruction and practice in choral music in his parish church of Saint Andrew, on which he had already spent the large sum for those days of £30,000. The money had paid for an almost complete rebuilding for which the architect was one of the central figures of the Victorian Gothic Revival, Sir Giles Gilbert Scott.

It is likely that either Scott or one of his office staff was responsible for designing the main buildings of the college which were erected in the 1850s and 60s. Stevens had been a close friend of Giles Gilbert Scott, himself an Anglican clergyman's son, since the 1830s and this friendship resulted in two marriages linking their families. Scott's daughter married the son of Thomas Stevens, while a daughter of Thomas Stevens married Scott's son John Oldrid Scott, who became an architect in his father's practice and was employed to design a number of the college buildings.

According to one account, Thomas Stevens "was himself the designer and chief architect" of these buildings. While it is very doubtful whether he actually provided the architectural drawings that would have been

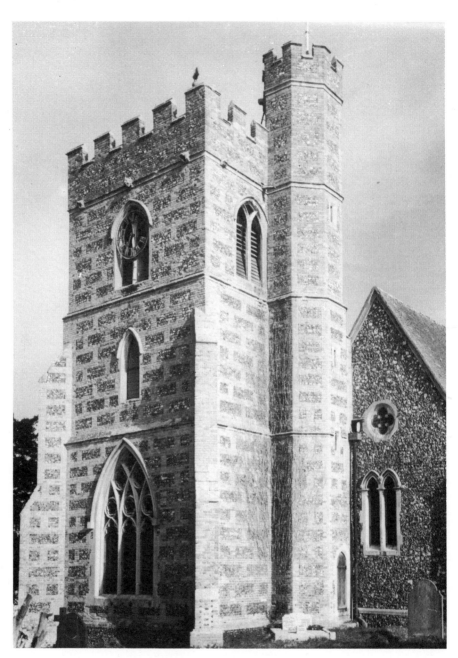

84. *14th century Bradfield Church Tower*

needed, he may well have had a decisive influence on what was put into execution, since Scott, in common with many of his contemporaries, always retained a highly respectful attitude towards landowners and wrote: "The position of a landed proprietor, be he squire or nobleman, is one of dignity . . . He is the natural head of his parish or district—in which he should be looked up to as the bond of union between the classes". At another point in his writing Scott also mentions the "strong will" of the College's founder and first Warden. It was a willpower that eventually failed to preserve Stevens from financial disaster when in 1881 he went bankrupt to the tune of £160,000. Though by that time the boys' quarters were infested with rats, the main buildings were complete. Those round the quadrangle incorporated parts of an old house, the walls and buttresses of a large barn and a many sided brick structure that may have been part of a late medieval gatehouse. A Dininghall was added in 1856 and a Hall, known as Big School, with a Library above it, in the 1860's and 1870's. These last three were designed by John Oldrid Scott, by this time a son-in-law of Warden Thomas Stevens.

Another son-in-law was a member of the glassmaking firm of Powell. It was this firm which in 1859 provided the splendid stained glass in the west window of the Dininghall to the designs of the young Burne-Jones. The window is in clear, bright colours, including some large areas in red, and forms a bold, striking composition which is a fine and characteristic example of Pre-Raphaelite art. Both the Dininghall and Big School are built in the Gothic style of the 13th century with narrow, pointed arched window lights. The impressive if slightly forbidding look of this range is enhanced by the flints which form the main walling, dressed with red bricks. This flintwork was no doubt a matter of conscious choice on the part of the architect, but it was also genuinely a case of using what was available locally, for a deep quarry only a short distance away was a source both of flints and of lime for mortar. The resultant hollow was adapted without difficulty in 1888 into an outdoor auditorium in which were given productions of Greek plays that continue to this day.

By 1892, after various changes of fortune, the College was found to have outgrown the parish church for which it was intended as an adjunct. A chapel was added to the south side of the quadrangle and was enlarged only ten years later by lengthening the chancel and adding a tower. The architect was, inevitably, John Oldrid Scott, who by this time had moved on from the 13th to the 14th century, with the result that his Gothic design is rather more lively and includes curving window tracery and arcades on columns of polished black plaster resembling marble. Altogether Bradfield College gives an excellent idea of the

85. Bradfield Church, interior

strength and some of the weaknesses of the Victorian Gothic Revival, with its emphasis on a return to the spirit of the Middle Ages in both architecture and religion. At its best, as in the window by Burne-Jones, it could inspire great artistic vigour and originality. But there was always a danger that medieval church architecture would be copied mechanically and employed on buildings for which it was not suited. Even in some of the school windows at Bradfield one can see that unhappy compromise of a Victorian plate glass sash window within a pointed stone arch.

While many of the Victorian landed gentry were patronising an architectural style which they regarded as essentially English, the great Whig magnates favoured a more international one which continued the European Renaissance tradition and can best be described as Italianate. At Cliveden, on a magnificent site overlooking a wooden stretch of the Thames, the Duke of Sutherland employed its ablest practitioner, Sir Charles Barry, to reconstruct the burnt out shell of a great country house. The history of the house before Barry took over is complicated, but briefly can be summarised as follows. In the reign of Charles II a Captain Wynne or Winde levelled two wide terraces, on the upper one of which he built a house for the Duke of Buckingham. In the early 18th century Thomas Archer, architect of Marlow Place, added wings on either side of the entrance court and connected them to the house by curved colonnades. A fire in 1795 gutted the house; it was restored in 1824 and burnt a second time in 1849. Barry built upon the foundations and followed the same general design but with taller proportions. The result is an unmistakably Victorian house with large, bold features in strong, hard stucco. Yet the block shape, roughly a double cube, is that of an earlier fashion and the arrangement of an arcaded ground floor and giant pilasters framing the two upper floors stems from 16th century Italy. The branching flights of steps leading down from the house to the lower terrace add to the impression of an Italian villa.

In 1893 Cliveden was bought by the immensely wealthy William Waldorf Astor. New York society had not accorded him the first place which he thought was his due and he determined to go one better by establishing himself in English society. No sooner had he bought Cliveden than he set about giving it an international, European character. In earlier times the Thames Valley had seen foreign materials, foreign styles and even foreign architects imported, but Astor was able to use his vast wealth to buy whole parts of European houses and transport them to England. From the Villa Borghese in Rome he brought the balustraded walls of the forecourt and placed them in front of the house on the lower

86. Cliveden, the north front from the fountain

terrace. The Italian courts had ruled that the balustrades were not works of art and so could be exported, but the statues at either end of the walls had to be left behind and copies were made to fill their places on the new site.

Astor also proceeded to order an almost complete remodelling of the interior of the house. For this he chose J. L. Pearson, an architect trained in the Victorian Gothic tradition who had designed an entire new cathedral at Truro. At first sight it was an odd choice of architect but Pearson, who went on to build an office and town house for Astor on the Victoria Embankment, was equal to the task. His entrance hall is an accomplished version of Carolean decoration, reasonably appropriate for the Brussels tapestries of a slightly later date which Astor bought without realising that they had once been at Cliveden and had been made for a previous owner of the house, Lord Orkney. The staircase leading off the hall has statuettes on the newel posts in the tradition of 17th century stairways at, for example, Hatfield House and Blickling Hall, but the figures at Cliveden, standing singly or in pairs, are typical of the late 19th century in being consciously historical. There are medieval knights, a cavalier and his lady, a Georgian gentleman with his wife, all of whom appear to have been taken from some country house charades. They are in fact supposed to represent characters in the history of the house. After this the hall chimneypiece, an early Renaissance importation from a 16th century French chateau, comes as a surprising, almost unmannerly, intrusion.

The centre of the main floor on the garden side has a fine drawing room. It contains a large French tapestry of the early to mid 18th century, that is to say from the first part of the reign of Louis XV. The rest of the decoration, however, is approximately Louis XVI (with an Empire chimneypiece), illustrating an odd vagueness characteristic of the late Victorians. Despite a strongly historical outlook, they were very often unconcerned about stylistic accuracy. Louis XV or Louis XVI, it was immaterial to them so long as the colours were light, the style more or less classical and the gilding lavish.

This historical approach was strongly characteristic of William Waldorf Astor. He was an amateur writer of novels and short stories set in the past, usually in France or in Italy, and some of his purchases for Cliveden reflect this taste for the more glamorous periods and characters in European history. From Madam de Pompadour's chateau at Asnières he imported a whole panelled room and had it fitted at Cliveden. A chimneypiece of 18th century chinoiserie design was inserted in one of the bedrooms, so that the house became a sort of anthology of the taste of

87. Cliveden, The Italian Tower

different countries and periods, rather in the same way as a book was formed out of his various historical romances, published first in the literary magazines which he founded and financed out of his enormous resources, the Pall Mall Magazine and the Pall Mall Budget. Indeed, in his town house on the Embankment, there were statues on the stairs representing characters taken from Astor's fictional writings.

The grounds at Cliveden have always been of the first importance as an architectural setting. Few of the various owners of the house have resisted the temptation to place buildings in them. The Duke of Buckingham for whom the first house was built had not much time to add garden structures, but the next purchaser, Lord George Hamilton, created Lord Orkney, employed the Venetian Giacomo Leoni to add two delightful garden pavilions. These are the Blenheim Pavilion, so named in honour of Orkney's part in that victory, and a small octagonal building transformed much later into a chapel. Leoni designed in a fairly restrained classical style in reaction to the earlier Baroque manner of Thomas Archer, architect of Marlow Place and of the now altered curving wings of the entrance front. It is interesting that Lord Orkney should have employed two architects working in different styles and shows how easily a change in architectural fashions could be accepted by people who were the political and social leaders of the country. Lord Orkney's wife certainly qualified as a leading member of English society, not only as a confidant of statesmen but also as hostess at Cliveden to both George I and George II.

In the mid 18th century Cliveden was rented by George II's son, Frederick Prince of Wales. He made no additions to the buildings but caused a clearing in the woods known as the Rustic Theatre to be used for concerts and musical entertainments. It was left to the Victorian owners of Cliveden, successively the Dukes of Sutherland, the Duke of Westminster and William Waldorf Astor, to add an extraordinary assortment of objects and structures. A small pagoda in the water garden came from the 1851 Exhibition. In 1861 the Duke of Sutherland ordered the construction of a stable block and clock tower by the architect Henry Clutton. He provided a design for the tower which takes the idea of a half open staircase from the French chateaux, but manages to look very mid Victorian. Another relic of the Sutherland period of ownership is the lead statue in the ilex grove of Prince Albert in a Highland kilt. His rather unexpected presence at Cliveden is due to the friendship of Queen Victoria with the Duchess of Sutherland and her frequent visits to the house and grounds.

Astor soon imported a more exotic collection of ornaments. For so

rich a man garden buildings were indeed no more than ornaments, but his main contribution was Roman and Italian sculpture. Flanking the entrance drive near the house and in the forecourt are eight carved Roman stone coffins, collected as works of art and regarded as so rare and valuable that it never apparently occurred to Astor that they might strike rather an unusual note of welcome to his guests. A similar disregard for the subject matter of works of art is to be found in the two statues in the Long Garden by the 18th century Venetian sculptor Giovanni Bonazza. As they represent an admiral of the Venetian fleet and the spirit of Navigation, they should by rights be nearer to some navigable water. But the spirit that really lingers at Cliveden is that of William Waldorf, first Viscount Astor, for he is buried in the chapel which his architect Pearson made out of Leoni's octagonal pavilion and decorated with mosaics.

CHAPTER VII
Conclusion

This survey of historic buildings in the Thames Valley has taken us through nine centuries. In each period from the Medieval to the Victorian it has been possible to point to an astonishing wealth and variety of architecture. In no other European country can one trace such a consistent, unbroken record of secular architecture in a comparatively small area, embracing both town and country dwellings. This continuous evidence of inventiveness and skill is only in part due to the fact that the region suffered from no foreign invasions and no serious destruction from civil strife. Neither the Wars of the Roses nor the Civil War had any widespread effect on the buildings of the countryside nor any lasting one on its prosperity.

In this respect the Thames Valley compares well with some other parts of England. The Cotswolds, for all the charm of its stone villages, suffered a form of architectural stagnation in the 17th century when the wool trade declined and the region lost much of its prosperity. It was not until this time that the north of England achieved enough wealth or sufficiently settled conditions near the Scottish border for the spread of lasting dwellings for most ranks of society. But in the Thames Valley there are still surviving examples of yeomen's houses from as early as the 14th century. Their descendants through succeeding centuries continued to build houses which remain to be a source of pride to their owners and of pleasure to the passing visitor.

This pleasure is not only due to the way these buildings fit their surroundings. Very often this is their least noticeable characteristic, a quality of which one may only become aware by contrast with some brash intrusion. Mellow stone and brickwork can blend into their surroundings, merging with garden walls and with outbuildings to form a continuous pattern. What may strike one more at first sight is the astonishing resourcefulness of these builders. As they adapted their native

skill to changing demands in successive ages, they showed at every turn a capacity for varying and improving on the techniques involved.

They were always prepared to venture on the use of fresh materials. Perhaps the most outstanding instance of this adaptability is their development of timber framing from quite simple beginnings in the early middle ages to the complex and ingenious houses of the 15th and 16th centuries. This gradual perfection of a technique that was both structural and decorative has no parallel outside England. Other English regions may have as good timber framing but they lack equal skill in another advanced form of construction. The builders and architects of the Thames Valley in the 17th and 18th centuries brought to brickwork in combination with stone the same attention to detail and the same overall sense of design. They were just as prepared to use fine woodwork or decorative plaster.

Nor is this an inbred architecture. Of all parts of England, the Thames Valley was one of the most receptive to new ideas and methods, whether from other regions or from abroad. What they borrowed they generally managed to adapt and transform to fit their native architecture. Nothing could surely be more essentially English than the timber framed Manor House at Ockwells, yet it incorporates stained glass, which had started as a French technique. The whole Renaissance style of architecture, originating in Italy, was subtly changed to suit English conditions.

Until quite recently these importations could be absorbed into a continuing native tradition. In the Victorian age came a lessening of distinctive regional character in architecture. The industrial revolution meant a great increase in the use of standardised materials. Small kilns gave way to large, so that bricks were brought from a distance. It became cheaper to get slates from Wales than to use local stone slates or tiles. From the large industrial towns came cast iron in many forms, for grates, balcony railings and roof crests, all mass produced in standard patterns.

The effect of this change was delayed for a time by a vigorous reaction. The Arts and Crafts movement of the late 19th century, centred on London and the Cotswolds, affected architecture as much as other arts. Architects such as Voysey and Lutyens built country houses in their own, often highly personal versions of traditional themes. Though deeply immersed in the architecture of the past, they yet achieved results which were both original and pleasing.

Since the last world war most architects have rejected past styles. Their use of a whole range of fresh materials, such as steel, concrete and aluminium, has given them a new freedom of design and at the same

time dealt a final death blow to English regional architecture. It is now possible to look back on nearly a thousand years of that architecture in the Thames Valley and to marvel at its achievement. If one tries to sum up this sequence of fine buildings, its three greatest assets are adaptability and fitness to surroundings, combined with a strong sense of form and design.

The last of these is to be expected anywhere in the houses of the rich and powerful. What is much more surprising and unusual is to find this artistic sense employed on the dwellings of ordinary yeomen farmers and even on barns and dovecotes. The same process can be noticed when one traces the evolution of different parts of buildings. What starts as purely functional, as a necessary unit in a structure, soon acquires a decorative quality of its own, whether it is a chimney stack, a new form of window or a section of timber framework. In looking at buildings which are in fact works of art, we can gain some insight into the lives of their past inhabitants, the nobles and gentry, the merchants, yeomen farmers and craftsmen of the Thames Valley.

HOUSES OPEN TO THE PUBLIC at certain times of the year:

Cliveden, near Taplow, Buckinghamshire
Greys Court, near Henley, Oxfordshire
Kingston House, Kingston Bagpuize, Berkshire (gardens only)
Mapledurham House, near Caversham, Oxfordshire
Milton Manor House, near Abingdon, Berkshire
Nuneham Park, Nuneham Courtney, Oxfordshire
Windsor Castle, Berkshire (state apartments)

INDEX

A Map of the THAMES VALLEY

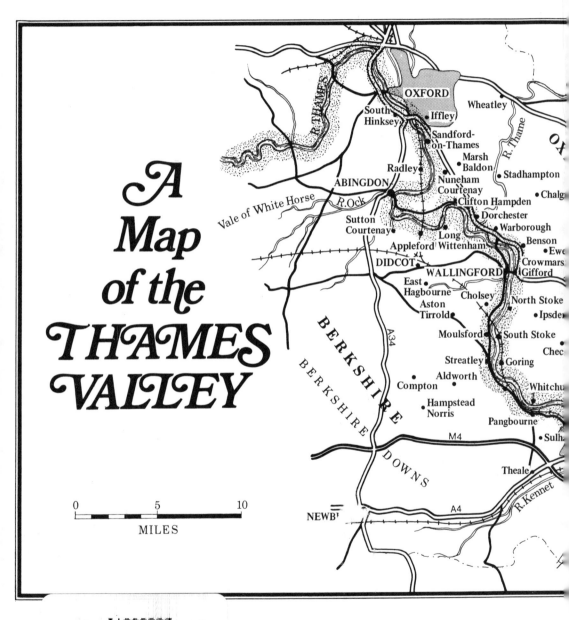

OXFORD
Wheatley
South Hinksey
Iffley
Sandford-on-Thames
R. Thame
R. THAMES
Marsh Baldon
Radley
Stadhampton
Nuneham Courtenay
ABINGDON
Chalg
Clifton Hampden
Vale of White Horse
R. Ock
Dorchester
Sutton Courtenay
Warborough
Appleford
Long Wittenham
Benson
Ewe
DIDCOT
Crowmars
WALLINGFORD
Gifford
East Hagbourne
Cholsey
North Stoke
Aston Tirrold
Ipsde
A34
Moulsford
South Stoke
Streatley
Chec
Goring
Aldworth
Compton
Whitchu
BERKSHIRE
Hampstead Norris
BERKSHIRE
Pangbourne
M4
Sulh
BERKSHIRE DOWNS
Theale
NEWB
A4
R. Kennet

OX

0   5   10
MILES

D085567I